M000234695

MY BELOVED COMMUNITY

MY BELOVED COMMUNITY

Sermons, Lectures and Speeches
of
Rev. Daughtry

REV. HERBERT D. DAUGHTRY, SR.

Africa World Press, Inc.

P.O. Box 1892
Trenton, NJ 08607

P.O. Box 48
Asmara, ERITREA

Africa World Press, Inc.

P.O. Box 1892
Trenton, NJ 08607

P.O. Box 48
Asmara, ERITREA

Book design: Wanjiku Ngugi & Elias A. Gebrezgheir
Cover design: Jonathan Gullery

Library of Congress Cataloguing-in-Publication Data

Daughtry, Herbert.
  My beloved community : sermons, speeches, and lectures / by Herbert D. Daughtry.
      p. cm.
Includes bilbiographical references and index.
    ISBN 0-86543-589-8 -- ISBN 0-86543-590-1 (pbk.)
  1. Sermons, American--African American authors. I. Title.
    BV4241.5 .D38 2001
    252--dc21

                                        2001002311

DEDICATION

To my family. My wife: Karen, children: Leah, Sharon, Dawn and Dan Dan and grandson, Rennie. I cannot imagine how my life would have been without you all. How blessed I am to have such a family. I love you all. And, I am so proud of each one of you individually, and collectively.

ACKNOWLEDGMENTS

As always, I start my acknowledgments with my relationship to God through Jesus Christ, my Lord and Savior. Always, I am grateful for all I have received and for all I have been allowed to give.

Then to my family, Dr. Karen Smith Daughtry, my wife, for her editorial, computer, and overall counsel; to my eldest daughter, Leah, the administrator, for her everything regarding the origin and summation of this volume. Without her assistance there would be no book.

To daughter Sharon, the artist, for her hugs and kisses of encouragement; to daughter Dawn, the preacher, for her encouragement and powerful preaching on the themes embodied in this book; to our son Herb Jr. (Dan Dan), the lawyer, for his legal advice and overall encouragement. To Rennie, my only grandson, just for being Rennie, intelligent, creative, loving, always trying to be helpful.

To the members of my church, whatever I am, whatever I have accomplished, they must share the success. I will take the criticism—what I am they help to make me.

To Robin Renaud, Laverne Walker, Pamela Mucherera, Yvonne Rubie, Minister Dorothy Isaac, Deacon Leroy Applin, Sharman Blake, Deborah Dawkins, Jackie Scott, and Amy Lou Council, one of my oldest members in point of service, all helped in some way to produce this volume.

To Dr. A.G. Miller, professor of church history, Oberlin College, our midwest district minister, whose prodding and sagacious insight across the years have always kept me moving ahead.

To Charles Barron, president and C.E.O. of Dynamics of Leadership, longtime friend and former chief of staff, for his encouragement and insights.

To my editor, Patricia Allen, the perfectionist, whose editorial skills are incomparable, for correcting my innumerable errors, and for giving clarity to my writing.

One of my reasons for writing is to give a place of recognition to the innumerable people who have struggled with me to make a better world, people who, for the most part, would never be recognized and/or appreciated for their contributions, and since I have been the direct and indirect beneficiary of their commitment I believe it is only right and proper that I say, Thank you, and to record their names for all the world to know who they are and what they contributed.

In the last volume there were people I failed to acknowledge who played a significant role in my life and struggles. I seek their indulgence and hope my attempt to make it up to them by including them in this volume is acceptable.

Oronde Takuma, who was with me in the early days of the Black United Front; Reverend Jew Don Boney, long-time friend and struggler; and finally my friend and mentor, the prodigious intellect, Dr. Cornel West, for his encouragement across the years and for writing the foreword of my last book *No Monopoly on Suffering*.

Eternal gratitude to Peggie Washington who led the boycott at the beginning of the our movement. Ditto for Zakiya Russ who joined us while pregnant, and the fruit of her womb, Dajanaba Bird, is now one of our young ministers.

Mr. Paul (Weusi) Washington, who sacrificed his political interest to act as my Chief of Security. I am sure he added years to my life, and my family as well, by relieving us of any stress related to my security.

CONTENTS

INTRODUCTION

THE BELOVED COMMUNITY

This book is a compilation of sermons, speeches, and lectures given over a period of years. The thoughts themselves, in one form or another, have been in my mind in various stages of development for a long time. I marvel that the ideas are still relevant, which leads me to the conviction that there is a timelessness about the thoughts; or as long as the issues I address are present, the analysis and suggested tactics for change will remain to some degree the same.

It seems that I have always been concerned with the well-being of my people. I realize it may sound excessively nationalistic, or absurd, or self-serving, but for as long as I can remember, I have been race conscious. When I was not yet ten years old, I worked for a Chinese grocery store in Augusta, Georgia. Eventually, I was fired for giving the Black customers too much merchandise for their money. I would deliberately overstuff their bags, give an extra pound of meat, anything to increase their lot. I felt I had to do something to help. Things just did not seem right; they never did. Blacks were always at the bottom and always treated disrespectfully. I did not understand why but I knew there was a difference.

Throughout my teen years and on into manhood, I maintained this sensitivity to racial conditions, no matter what else was occupying my time. I was aware, albeit superficially, of our state of affairs. Always, subjects related to Black history or struggle or social conditions would capture my interest. So it followed naturally that once I had committed my life to Jesus Christ, my racial concerns and religious convictions would merge—my history and theology would be complimentary, or I would seek to express each one in the others garb.

It is not only for my needs that I merge African history and struggle with my religion, but, again for my people's sake. Christianity had fallen on hard times in the Black communities of the world. It was viewed as the white man's "trick bag" to keep us blind and subservient, docile and accommodating, or it was a panacea, putting us to sleep or making us dream about heaven while he, the white man, was taking everything on earth. The Black intelligentsia and or bourgeois did not think it was worth debating any longer. They had long since out grown the religion of their youth. In the church, Black businessmen saw only dollar signs; Black politician saw only votes.

I felt an irresistible urge to emphasize the reality of God through Jesus Christ, who could be experienced in a personal way, and that the Bible is the work of God, and when interpreted rightly will lead us to truth. We could live purposeful, relevant, healthy, happy, productive lives on earth and still look forward to heaven. The time-tested religious exercises of prayer, fasting, Bible reading, faith sharing, regular church attendance, consistent service, and disciplined life styles were of paramount value. In addition, I felt compelled to express that personal faith, that fundamental biblical Christianity in relevant, historical, sociological, and political terms.

Especially for African people, it was necessary to show the Africaness of Christianity, and the years of struggle in which those of our people who were Christians have been engaged. This had to be done without losing the universal character of Christianity. To do so would be to end up with a race religion, and that would not be Christian. At the very heart of Christianity is the teaching, the fatherhood of God and the brotherhood of man—or the familyship of all people. God so loved the world that he gave His only begotten Son . . . .

There is a separation. It is on the basis of faith. God extends an open hand to everyone, but God does not force anyone. The decision is left to humanity. Those who are Christians are so because they chose to be. Those who are not, choose not to be. Race, class, birth has nothing to do with it. "We are saved by faith." It is a gift of God and not of works . . . says the Bible.

The challenge, then, is how to deepen personal faith in a personal God and express it both in personal ways and in political, historical, collective ways. How can one emphasize the cultural and the cosmopolitan simultaneously? Or how can one love one's people and love the world at the same time? There were several scriptures which were helpful.

> Jesus said to his disciples, "Go not into the way of the Gentiles, and into any City of the Samaritans enter ye not" (Matthew 9:5,6).

> "But he answered and said, I am not sent but unto the lost sheep of the house of Israel" (Matthew 15:24).

And the Apostle Paul wrote:

> Though I might also have the confidence in the flesh. If any other man thinketh that he hath whereof he might trust in the flesh, I more:

> Circumcised the eighth day, of the stock of Israel, of the tribe of Benjamin, a Hebrew of the Hebrews; as touching the law, a Pharisee;

> Concerning zeal, persecuting the church; touching the righteousness which is in the law, blameless.

> But what things were gain to me, those I counted loss for Christ. (Phillipians 3:4,7).

When we study these scriptures, we observe that Jesus and Paul are saying, I must first deal with me, and my people where we are. Then we can go beyond cultural considerations. Jesus first said, my ministry is confined to "the Lost Sheep of the House of Israel." But later he said, "Go ye into all the world and teach all Nations . . ." (Matthew 28:13-20). Clearly, then Jesus starts at home and moves to encompass the world. Likewise, Paul begins with his cultural credentials, then moves to a more comprehensive affirmation. "What things were gained to me, those I counted loss for Christ." We can transcend culture when we have given proper respect to culture. The approach of Jesus and Paul allow room for cultural appreciation within a universal content.

You may be African, Irish, Italian, or whatever, and love your people and your culture, and at the same time be a part of the total human experience with love and appreciation. That is the universal principle, from the natural to the spiritual, from the cultural to transcendence. Too often there is an attempt to degrade or distort the history of a people. Those who come to power through oppression and exploitation know that one of the ways to sustain themselves in power is to remove from the minds of those whom they oppress any link to past greatness and accomplishment, and since religious people often times become the handmaidens of slavers, colonizers, exploiters, they try to put God on their side.

With that bit of background, I spent considerable time reading, thinking, writing, speaking, always searching for the biblical, relevant merger. What follows in this book is a token of that labor. It is my religious creed, which, succinctly stated, is:

> I believe in God the Father, maker of all things, who is no respecter of person, and in Jesus Christ, his only begotten son, who was uniquely anointed to manifest God and to redeem humanity.

> I believe that Jesus was essentially African in origin. While Abraham, the father was located in Asia, still hundreds of years in Egypt, Northern Africa (and Canaan) in which obvious assimilation of religion, philosophy, medicine, art, architecture, engineering, etc. occurred, what was passed on to Jesus was Africaness - and while there was an assimilation of many other cultures, i.e., Assyrian, Babylonian, Persian, Syriann, Greek, Roman, it still remains that the essential foundation of Jesus was African. Moreover, even these assimilated cultures had come under the influence of Africa.

> I believe that in his redemptive work Jesus identified with and focused his ministry primarily towards the poor, sick, powerless and rejected.

> I believe He employed different methods in His redemptive work.

> I believe His very person and work (and also His servants

in every age) produced an inevitable conflict with societal rulers. Jesus' redeeming work creates a new person, who in turn constitutes, a new society whose interest, value, morals, mores are/were in direct conflict with systems and rulers of this world.

I believe that God, the Father, and Jesus Christ, through the Holy Spirit, call, fill, and send human beings of every nationality, gender, class, and age to continue the ministry of Jesus Christ.

I believe that Jesus will come again, as He promised. While it is not absolutely clear what this means, I believe that when Jesus returns, there will be a dramatic, supernatural in-break, into history, and at that point a new heaven and new earth will begin in which peace and righteousness will flourish.

I believe that scientific discovery, space exploration and political and economic revolutions are all part of the divine plan in which God through Jesus Christ is at work moving all things toward His consummation.

Here is my mission statement, with implementation, which I wrote for my church many years ago.

The mission of The House of the Lord Church is to apply the Gospel of Jesus Christ in a holistic synthesis of progressive spiritual and social action, including:

- Personal salvation through Jesus Christ, the filling and in-dwelling of the Holy Ghost, healing for body and mind, high moral and ethical disciplines, and the return of Jesus Christ.

- A struggle against all forms of oppression and exploitation—often manifested as racism, sexism, and classism.

- A struggle for human rights and self-determination for all people.

To implement this holistic approach, our ministry includes:

- *Priestly*: Interceding with God through prayer, fasting, ritual, and ceremony.
- *Pastoral*: Providing healing, counseling and direction.
- *Prophetic*: Critiquing society from a biblical perspective, which places God on the side of the oppressed, exploited, outcasts, and impoverished.
- *Pedagogic*: Teaching not only the great truth of scripture, but also secular history, particularly the truths related to oppressed people's contribution to humankind.
- *Programmatic*: Developing education, cultural, social, and economic programs and institutions.
- *Political*: Creating and/or participating in the creation of organizations and/or coalitions, that employ various actions to achieve human fulfillment.

To this initial list I have since added two more:

- *Health*: I believe it is God's will that we enjoy optimum health. In III John 1:2, these words are recorded, "I would above all that you may prosper and be in good health, even as your soul prospers."
- *Develop Human Potential*: Jesus said, "The Kingdom of God is within you." This means that there is limitless potential slumbering within every human being.

In essence, it is these five pillars which undergird my ministry and my mission:

- Personal Salvation
- The struggle for human rights and self-determination
- The importance of history and culture
- Optimum health
- Tapping the power within

Toward that end every Sunday, I insert a four-sided pastoral sheet into the church's bulletin. The front gives the title. The left inside panel: "Soul and Spirit" deals with matters related to the world of "spirit and mind." The inside right panel deals with health issues;

every week there is an article regarding health. The back panel deals with "Race and Politics." On this side, I have addressed myriad political, social, and historical issues.

Finally, inevitably there are repetitions. Speeches that were made over such a long period of time and in many different places would necessarily include repetition. Ideas are like children. If properly nurtured, they are always evolving. What is said in one place is expanded in another.

At any rate, to take the quote from a speech may destroy the essence and the continuity of said speech. So better to stay with the repetition. In addition, repetition promotes memorization.

This book is divided into four chapter:

Chapter I discusses my theology of liberation. It is the study of God in relation to violence, oppression, liberation and history. There are two lectures in this chapter.

The lecture "The Beloved Community" was originally prepared for and delivered at a 1972 Martin Luther King, Jr. program at Brooklyn's Zion Baptist Church, which was pastored by Dr. Benjamin Lowery. It was later expanded for The Black Liberation Revival, a program sponsored by the Chicago Chapter of the National Black United Front in 1982, and a Martin Luther King, Jr. program sponsored by the students at the University of Massachusetts in 1983.

"The Theology of Black Liberation, the What, Who, and How" was a lecture delivered at the Protestant Episcopal Theological Seminary in Virginia in 1973 on its 105th anniversary. The lecture attempts to talk about liberation and God's role in it.

Chapter II is my analysis of social, historical, political developments from my religious perspective.

"Threat from the New Right, Tracing the History of an Old Wrong" was delivered to a conference on the Constitution in Charleston, West Virginia, in May 1982.

"History of Racism" was delivered in October 1993 at the YWCA in Brooklyn. With substantial help from J.A. Rogers book *Africa's Gift to America*, I seek to pinpoint the origin of racism.

Chapter III offers some solutions, tactics, and strategies for change.

"Strengthening the Black Community" was delivered in 1992 to the Black Issues Convention of New Jersey in Newark, New Jersey. The Black Issues Convention is chaired by Councilman Donald Tucker.

"From Victims to Victors: Responding Creatively to Change In the City" was delivered in 1992 to the Reformed Church in America at Marble Collegiate Church in New York.

Chapter IV is my Christological statement. There are two parts in this section: The first, "Jesus: African in Origin, Revolutionary and Redeeming in Action," was first delivered in 1980 at the Harvard University School of Divinity and was expanded in 1984 at Cornell University's Sage Chapel. It is an attempt to validate the African origin of Jesus and His concerns for the whole person. It grapples with the question, What would Jesus do in any situation. This is an age of revolution. What would Jesus do today? How and where would He conduct His ministry?

The second part of this chapter is a series of sermons entitled "Jesus: The Surprising Contemporary," preached at the House of the Lord Pentecostal Church and on the radio station WWRL during the year 1972. These sermons take a more traditional approach. The Jesus discussed here, for the most part, is the Jesus of fundamental Christianity. I am indebted to William Barclay whose book, *Crucified and Crowned,* I drew upon heavily.

CHAPTER ONE

PART I
THE BELOVED COMMUNITY

PART II
THEOLOGY OF BLACK LIBERATION

THE BELOVED COMMUNITY
A HISTORICAL OVERVIEW OF BLACK CHURCH
MEN AND WOMEN'S STRUGGLE FOR FREEDOM

The subtitle of this presentation makes it clear that when I reflect on the beloved community, I'm thinking primarily, although not exclusively, of church men and women of African ancestry.

Martin Luther King would probably think differently of the beloved community. His emphasis would probably be black and white togetherness: "Little black boys and girls joining hands with little white boys and girls as sisters and brothers." While I would give a hearty amen to his shining idealism, what troubles me is that we have not yet reached the point of Black unity and pride where Black boys and girls join hands with Black boys and girls as brothers and sisters. And in the absence of that bond, the benefit of "joining hands" with other folks is unclear. To be sure, we must ever be striving for universal brotherhood and sisterhood, ever be building coalitions for freedom struggles, but if people of African ancestry are fragmented and bereft of racial pride, what will this universal togetherness and coalition mean for them?

It is my contention that every nationality must first address its own or at the least be equal in addressing the needs of its own while trying to fit into the universal mosaic. This is particularly true where there have been attempts to destroy the self-respect and history of a people.

If I am not for myself, to paraphrase Rabbi Hillel, who will be for me, and if I'm only for myself, who am I? Even Jesus said to his disciples, "First go to the lost sheep of the House of Israel" (Matthew 10:5, 6). Later he would say, "Go ye therefore and teach all nations," (Matthew 28:19) and then again, "Ye shall be witnesses unto me both in Jerusalem, and in all Judea and in Samaria, and unto the uttermost part of the world" (Acts 1:8).

With that bit of introduction, I want to discuss five periods of Black church men and women's history since the slave ships landed in the wilderness of North America.

Bear in mind that these five periods are very loosely defined. Actually, the flow of history can never be rigidly caught into nice, neat compartments. One period of history flows into another, sometimes imperceptibly; for convenience sake, we chop history into segments.

So, for my purposes, and convenience I have set out five periods of Black church history, and I will try to lay out and interpret a tiny piece of important reality during each. The five periods are:

1. A Time of Rebellion	(??? - 1864)
2. A Time of Relief	(1865 - 1880)
3. A Time of Retreat	(1880 - 1955)
4. A Time of Revival	(1955 - 1968)
5. A Time of Reaffirmation	(1968 - 1990)

There were two elements that shaped the Black church: the European-Christian influence and the African influence.

While the European influence is universally known, the African input is seldom recognized. A strong argument can be made for the African origin of Christianity itself. Perhaps that is one of the reasons slaves so readily accepted the slave master's religion. It really wasn't the slave master's but the slaves.[1]

These two influences fused together to create a religion that was peculiarly African American. The slave, taking from the slave master what is sometimes called the Judeo-Christian religion, infused it with the ancient rhythm, religion, and tradition of his progenitors, and created a new or different brand of Christianity or so broadened its dimensions as to make it applicable to the slave situation at that time.

W.E.B. DuBois wrote: "This church was not at first by any means Christian nor definitely organized; rather it was an adaptation and mingling of heathen rites among the members of each plantation, and roughly designated as Voodooism. Association with the masters, missionary effort and motives of expedience gave these rites an early veneer of Christianity, and after the lapse of many generations the Negro church became Christian."[2]

It was the "religion of the folk," as Joseph Washington called it in his book *Black Religion,*[3] or the "invisible church," as E. Franklin Frazier called it in his book *The Negro Church in America,*[4] that sustained African Americans in the awful years of slavery. It was the Black church which provided a teleology—a purposefulness; a theology—an understanding of God in relationship to slavery; a cosmology—a world view; an eschatology—an understanding of the future. It was the Black church that gave to the world the Black preacher, especially the slave or field preacher. This preacher was a unique character. His function was to heal, to comfort, and, yes, even to lead rebellions. DuBois wrote, regarding the early Black preacher during the early days of slavery:

> It was a terrific social revolution, and yet some traces were retained of the former group life, and the chief remaining institution was the Priest or Medicine man. He early appeared on the plantation and found his function as the healer of the sick, the interpreter of the unknown, the comforter of the sorrowing, the supernatural avenger of wrong, and the one who rudely but picturesquely expressed the longing, disappointment, and resentment of a stolen and oppressed people. Thus, as bard, physician, judge and priest, within the narrow limits allowed by the slave system, rose the Negro preacher and under him the first Afro-American Institution, the Negro church.[5]

A TIME OF REBELLION (??? -1864)

Consider, first, a time of rebellion. It should be clearly understood that rebellion here means confrontation against or defiance of an unjust system. Observe three characteristics of this rebellion:

1. Emigration;
2. The Underground Railroad; and
3. Insurrection.

Emigration

During the early years of slavery, there were multitudes of Black people who believed that the evils of American institutions could never be eradicated. Therefore, emigration was the only answer. However, there were others who believed that the struggle should be waged on two fronts—emigration as well as resistance within the boundaries of the U.S.A.—thus giving birth to the spirit of nationalism and Pan-Africanism, of self-determination and Black power, namely:

The Reverend Henry Highland Garnett, who questioned the presence of white leadership in the Black struggle, 120 years before SNCC and the Congress of Racial Equality (CORE); Martin Delaney, physician, author and journalist, who worked for a time with Frederick Douglass on the *North Star*, constructive colonizer in the Niger Valley; The erudite and stately Reverend Alexander Crummel; The Reverend Theodore Holly, who traveled to Haiti in search of freedom, carrying with him many brave and venturesome souls; Bishop Richard Allen, the torch bearer, the way-shower; and finally, the undaunted Bishop Daniel Coker. After the Civil War, to that illustrious body were added the names of Edward Wilmot Blyden, the scholar and theoretician; the angry, strident, fearless Bishop McNeil Turner; and the learned Bishop James Hood, to name but a few who sowed the seeds of emigrationalism, nationalism, and Black pride, which at the turn of the twentieth century produced the "Back to Africa" movement of Marcus Garvey and the "Pan-Africanism" of W.E.B. DuBois; Bishop Alexander Walters and George Padmore; the Black Power ideas of Stokely Carmichael and Floyd McKissick in the Sixties; the Black Theology of James Cone; the reparations idea of James Forman and Queen Mother Moore; and the independent Black Institution concept of Jitu Weusi and Preston Wilcox.

Perhaps more than anyone, Martin Delaney spoke for those seekers of the freedom beyond the sea. He put forth two ideas that will be with us as long as time itself.

Forever enshrined in the consciousness (albeit in the unconsciousness of too many) of Black people is the idea that we are a noble people, a great and generous people, destined by the Creator to usher in a new, higher order of civilization; and that this divine work cannot be accomplished in the U.S.A., rather we have been called to return to the fatherland.

Delaney strained with all his might to give our suffering and injustice a theology, that is, seeing in it all as God's plan to enlighten us and strengthen us and then to return us to our homeland where we would build the great civilization.

The Underground Railroad

Another attempt to escape from slavery was the creation of the Underground Railroad, which ran from the deep South to Canada. Slaves, making their escape, found persons who would assist them along the way, risking everything to help. The Black church was very much involved. It charted the routes, provided the funds, the food, and the clothing. It marked out the stops and rallied support from sympathizers. It developed and perfected the code, a means of communication, the most notable of which we have come to call spirituals. Unarguably the sweet, sad songs of the slaves conveyed a message other than that suggested on the surface. "Steal Away to Jesus" surely meant just what it said; steal away to Jesus in quiet prayer. But it also meant steal away to the secret gathering where plans were made for escape.

Insurrection

The Third, and most dramatic characteristic of the rebellion, saw the Black church as the vehicle that initiated (in some instances) and sustained (in other instances) violent insurrections. Desperate people are driven to desperate actions. Violence begets violence, and the violence employed by whites to perpetuate black enslavement inevitably evokes a violent reaction.

The three most famous violent insurrections were those led by Gabriel Prosser, Denmark Vesey, and Nat Turner. In 1800, Gabriel Prosser, then around the age of 16, holding forth the image of Samson as his hero, drew up plans whereby he would start an insurrection in Virginia which would extend across America. He would establish a nation of free black men on the North American continent. Obviously, Gabriel had been influenced by Toussaint L'Overture, who had led the first successful revolution against slavery in the New World. But poor Gabriel, like many others before him and after him, was betrayed by his own brothers in bondage.

Denmark Vesey's plan was even more ambitious than Gabriel's. Denmark had enlisted somewhere between three and nine thousand Blacks who stood ready to move at the right time. The area of operation was Charleston, South Carolina. The date was set, July 14, 1822, later changed to June 16. But again, brothers in bondage betrayed him and the insurrection never came off. It is significant that the Hempstead Methodist church was so involved in the plot that it was disbanded after the failure of the insurrection.

An even more well-known insurrection is that of Nat Turner, a Virginia slave and a Baptist preacher. Turner, like Gabriel and Vesey before him, saw visions from on high and applied scripture according to his own understanding of what God was saying to him and his people in their situation. After the death and destruction of 57 whites in a twenty mile area in the South Hampton County in Virginia, Nat Turner, along with 53 other Blacks, was arrested and tried. Twenty-one were acquitted, twelve transported out of the state, and twenty—Nat Turner among them—hanged.[6]

These three leaders personified the liberation aspirations of the Black church during those years of slavery. There were many more insurrections other than the slave master would have us believe. This can be construed from the numerous references to prohibition against Black religious assemblage. It was a known fact among the slave masters in those days that Black preachers were instigators of insurrections, and that the church was the meeting place of plots and schemes and strategies to escape, to confront, and to rebel. W.E.B. DuBois wrote of the Nat Turner insurrection:

> A wave of legislation passed over the South prohibiting the slaves from learning to read and write, forbidding Negroes to preach and interfering with Negroes religious meetings. Virginia, declared in 1831, that neither slaves nor free Negroes might preach nor could they attend religious services at night without permission. In North Carolina, slaves and free Negroes were forbidden to preach, exhort, or teach in any prayer meeting or other association for worship slaves of different families are collected together on penalty of not

more than thirty-nine lashes. Maryland and Georgia had similar laws. The Mississippi law of 1831 said, It is unlawful for any slave, free Negro, or mulatto to preach the gospel upon pain of receiving thirty-nine lashes upon the naked back of the presumptuous preacher. . . .[7]

Rebellion

Governor John Floyd of Virginia wrote:

> From all that has come to my knowledge during and since this affair, I am fully convinced that every black preacher in the whole county east of the Blue Ridge, was in on the secret.[8]

In Louisiana, the editor of the *Baton Rouge Gazette* wrote:

> We need not wonder if deeds of blood and murder should take place if incendiary preachers are allowed to hold forth with impunity at camp meetings and other places where our slaves congregate, and boldly make appeals to the worst passions of human nature.
>
> A stop must be put to the ranting and raving of these wolves in sheep's clothing.[9]

How strange that the editor of the *Baton Rouge Gazette* should call the desire for freedom, "The worst passion of human desire." South African poet Duma Ndlovu has a poem in which he underscores the atrocities of the Apartheid regime in South Africa and then dramatically pointing to himself he exclaims, "And they say I'm the terrorist!" The lesson, of course, is that those who struggle for freedom and/or what is right must disregard their oppressors or those who enjoy the status quo's definitions of reality and define themselves and their actions. The pharaohs of the world will always call the Moses of the world terrorists.

One of the ways to define power is the ability to define reality and make it acceptable to the world. When Jesse Jackson was running for the presidency of the United States, early on we decided we would determine what winning was. For example, we didn't think we would win the presidential election. But we knew we would involve countless people in the political process and the fallout would be immeasurable.

Europeans have defined reality by setting the European standard for everything. They said white skin was better than black; straight hair better than thick; individualism better than collectivism. They said money was the standard means against which everything was evaluated or judged. They said Europe was paradise, Africa was a jungle of savages. They said they were destined to rule and they made it happen. The humanity of color accepted or pretended they did. Europeans developed the power to force their will and definitions upon the rest of the world.

Enough has been said to demonstrate indisputably that the African-American church was very much involved in the freedom movement of that time; it was a church which had liberation on its mind. We will have to agree with Gay Wilmore, who writes in his book *Black Religion and Black Radicalism*:

> Thus, from David Walker [whose famous writings called "Walker's Appeal" urged slaves to take up arms], to Nat Turner, Black religion in the United States, strongly fortified by the Old Testament apocalyptic, provided the slaves with the inner resources to resist oppression, with violence if necessary. The white people of the south who observed the slave preachers at close range and knew of the fierce amalgam of African spirituality and radical Christianity which infused their sometimes open, but more often secret subversion of the slave system, threw up the ramparts of repressive legislation and the lynch laws against them.[10]

Perhaps it is best said in the old spiritual:

> Oh freedom, oh freedom, oh freedom over me
> And before I'll be a slave
> I'll be buried in my grave
> And go home to my Lord and be free.

We sing it differently today:

> Before I'll be a slave
> I bury the slave master in his grave
> And send him to hell
> So he can be with the devil.

A Time of Relief (1865 – 1880)

Consider now the years from 1865 to 1880. This is the period in which the chief characteristic of the church was relief. With the end of the Civil War, expectations were high. Surely Black people's slave days were over. Black people had agitated for years on the evils of slavery, creating over 50 antislavery societies. The country, it would seem, had come to accept that position. Black people had fought on behalf of the Union. In fact, it was said that there would have been no Union, for without the Black soldier the South would have won the war. Abraham Lincoln said as much. Not only that, but some people remembered that Blacks had also fought in the Revolutionary War 90 years before. It was Crispus Attacks whose blood was first spilled. Had the Black soldier not been at the barricades during those revolutionary days in the early history of this country, had they not been at Bunker Hill, Valley Forge, and Concord, there would have been no nation. George Washington said as much. And some remembered that Blacks had fought in the War of 1812 also.

So there was great anticipation. The days of bondage were over. Freedom and justice were begun. Long live the Union! Political gains enhanced the hope still more. The legislatures of the South had ample Black representation; from the State of Mississippi came two Black U.S. Senators, Hiram R. Revels and Blanche K. Bruce. In 1866, Congress passed the Civil Rights Bill over the veto of President Johnson. In 1875, more civil rights laws were enacted, and there were the constitutional safeguards: the 13th, 14th, and 15th Amendments to the Constitution.

So the Black church turned its attention away from rebellion toward relief efforts. The freed man needed special help to adjust to the new state of things and the gains made before the Civil War needed to be consolidated. With the generous assistance of white churches, schools were started, and burial societies grew into insurance companies. As John Hope Franklin wrote in his book *From Slavery to Freedom*:

> Another agency that offered both spiritual and material relief during Reconstruction was the Negro church. The end of the war led to the expansion of the independent churches among Negroes. There were no longer southern laws to

> silence Negro preachers and to proscribe their separate or-
> ganization. Negroes began to withdraw from white churches
> once they had secured their freedom and consequently the
> Negro church grew rapidly after the war.[11]

While the African American church was engaged in relief it also participated in the electoral process.

In the area of politics, the presence of the Black preacher has been and is still being felt. Of the 20 representatives from the south during the Reconstruction period, two were preachers. The first Black Senator, Hiram R. Revels, who was elected to the seat previously held by Jefferson Davis, was an AME pastor.

In the South Carolina Constitutional Convention, held January 14, 1868, of the 124 delegates, 78 were Black, and of that number 13 were ministers, about one-sixth of the total. And it was a Black minister, Richard H. Cain, who was elected to be one of the state's four congressmen.[12]

But the rosy picture was soon shattered. The hooded racists of the South began to ride, spreading terror and death and destruction. By the turn of the century, the nation had experienced another radical change, and the high hopes ushered in with the Civil War were dashed to the ground. The road the country had decided to take with the election of Rutherford B. Hayes in 1876 was quite clear. A compromise was struck wherein the white South agreed to the election of the aforementioned pusillanimous president, in exchange for which they would regain their autonomy, and that meant that Blacks would be theirs do with as they pleased. And they were pleased to bomb and lynch Black people into a state of servile submission.

The Ku Klux Klan and all the conspicuous racists of the South, along with the inconspicuous, conniving racists of the North, created a rigid pattern of segregation that reached the ludicrous heights of having separate toilets, all of which was supported by the sanctity of law. By the first decade of the twentieth century, all the lawmaking bodies of the South had succeeded in ousting Black representation and had set up legal mechanisms to prevent them from ever re-entering. Segregation had become the law of the land.

A Time of Retreat (1880 - 1954)

With the end of Reconstruction, the black church, faced with what appeared to be insurmountable obstacles, retreated or turned within. It still engaged in relief, but the singular characteristic of the church at this time was surrender, escapism, or institutional maintenance. It was a church retreating from the battle.

White philanthropists and churches played a significant role in the affairs of Black people during this time. Especially was this influence strong in the Black church. One of the places in which white influence was strongest was in the area of education. White school teachers went south to teach. These white churches and philanthropists raised money to build Black colleges. Because of this, some influence over Black life was the necessary consequence. This might have been one of the contributing factors in the Black church relinquishing its confrontational posture.

In many instances, this white influence sought to make Black churches over in the image of white churches. They tried to remove the emotionalism or demonstrative nature of the Black church's rituals and ceremonies, to reshape the decorum and language of the Black preacher, and to recast the hermeneutic and theology. Many whites (probably most) frowned on the peculiarity of the Black church. But they had a deeper reason for wanting to change it: They feared it and resented its independence. The Black preacher, the theology, the worship style and values are what made it different. And these elements are what created and fueled its freedom flame.

Into the great ocean that was the Black church flowed many religious streams from Africa—African traditional religion, Voodoo and Shangoism. Whites were alien to this experience. They could not understand it and wanted no part of it. What they did understand only too well was that from this source came Black people's insatiable desire and irresistible determination to be proud, independent, and free.

Mention has already been made of Prosser and Turner, who mingled Christianity and African traditional religions and/or symbolisms. One graphic example is the Maroons in Jamaica, who drew on their African religious heritage which inspired their rebellion. They defeated the slave masters and fought their way to freedom. There is a saying attributed to them, "Me no send, you no go!" Last I heard they were still in the hills of Jamaica, still free!

Now observe a very significant development. Because the church was retreating or turning within, it left a vacuum in the lives of Black people into which rushed five very interesting movements.

First, there was the Civil Rights Movement, starting with the Niagara Movement begun by W.E.B. DuBois in 1905, out of which came the National Association for the Advancement of Colored People (NAACP). Then there was the National Urban League (NUL) and the Congress of Racial Equality (CORE).

Second, there was the Nationalist Movement, initiated by Marcus Garvey, who must be considered the most renowned exponent of that time, perhaps of all time.

Third, there was the emergence of the Christian Sects. The Pentecostal preacher named Charles Seymour was one notable example.

Fourth, there was the Father Divine Peace Movement, which made lofty claims and fed hungry stomachs in the Father Divine Peace Kitchens. Bishop Grace or Sweet Daddy Grace, as he came to be called by his idolizing followers, would be included in this category.

And fifth, into the vacuum came the Islamic variations, the Moorish Science, Noble Drew Ali, and Master Fard Muhammad, from whom came the Nation of Islam of Elijah Muhammed.

It was as if Black people were frantically seeking something that would fill the void created by the church's abdication from its historic role.

It is worth noting that all the forms of religion—and this can be said of the Nationalist Movement as well—were primarily engaged in journeys either inward or upward, not in assaults against institutional evils. Churches were looking to hope coming from the sky and nationalist movements were looking across the ocean or both were engaged in "navel gazing." The task of confrontation was borne by the Civil Rights Movement, albeit marginally, which raised questions regarding the legality of segregated laws. In other words, these civil rights groups were the ones who sought to turn the system around or make a dent in it.

The impression should not be conveyed that there were no churches or churchmen engaged in confrontation. There were congregations here and there that continued in the fight, and there were preachers who kept swinging away. Sometimes they were alone, but they kept at it. There was Bishop Henry McNeil Turner, whose fiery voice and courageous posture held forth the true picture of the Black preacher during the latter part of the nineteenth century and the early part of the twentieth century; and of course, there was Adam Clayton Powell, Jr., who (while the behavior of his later years raised eyebrows) was on the street marching for better jobs and living conditions back in the early 1940s. With but a few exceptions, the Black church from 1880 to 1954 was non-confrontational, non-prophetic.

A Time For Revival (1955 - 1968)

In 1955 a strange thing happened. Looking back it seems so small, so insignificant, and yet the archives of history are replete with examples of mighty movements precipitated by the most minute incidents.

Rosa Parks decided that she was not going to get up and give her seat to a white man. When she sat down, a people stood up. Well, the story has been told too often to repeat here. Ms. Parks went to jail, and to her rescue came a small group of people, but that was not the end. It was, in fact the beginning of a new day. The insult was too much to take without retaliating. Something had to be done. When plans were laid to boycott the bus company, we were beginning to enter into the new phase of Black church history. To whom would the mantle of leadership fall in this battle? To a minister, who else? To whom have Black people ever turned in the hour of deepest despair and direst need? Who else has been called on when a Moses is needed? Who else but a Black minister.

And in that hour Dr. Martin Luther King, Jr., a young minister, came forward to lead the people of Montgomery. But he came forward to do much more. He came forward to resurrect the black church, the beloved community, and thus we found ourselves in the period of the Black church's revival. Dr. King came in the spirit of the early churchmen; in the spirit of the slave preacher or the preachers of the slave era. It was the spirit of confrontation. Through his organization, the Southern Christian Leadership Conference (SCLC), he was ready to challenge injustice and exploitation everywhere.

Most assuredly all churches didn't get involved. Maybe most didn't. Some had retreated so far that they didn't even know what was happening. Others had become so assimilated into everything white that they no longer thought of themselves as part of the "folk." Still others, even further back, stood in the distance and hurled stones of criticism. Why not pray and wait? Why not trust God? Why not be patient? The whole church was certainly not aroused, but a great number shook off the slouch of retreat and joined the march and went to the barricades, and even further, some went to their deaths.

The terms for the church's strategy changed occasionally. Sometimes it was called direct action; sometimes, noncompliance with evils; sometimes, selective buying; sometimes, nonviolent protest; sometimes, mass demonstration. Whatever the name, the meaning was clear: No more retreating.

To the eternal credit of Dr. Martin Luther King, Jr., the old banner of the Black church was raised up high, and given enough time and distance, when historians can accurately assess the legacy of this man, it might be recorded that his greatest contribution was that he revived the Black church from its slumber, calling it back from its retreat.

They will note the gains: The Voting Rights Bill of 1964 and 1965; the eradication of the legal underpinnings of discrimination and segregation; and the dignity and "somebodiness," now enjoyed by oppressed people from the struggle for justice.

All of these and others are the fruit of the sacrifice, toil, and blood of Black church men and women.

A Time of Reaffirmation (1968 – 1990)

With the death of Dr. Martin Luther King the church found itself in the midst of a volcanic upheaval and an insistence on Afrocentricity. For over 20 years now, the old ship of Zion has had to make its way through the stormy seas without the leadership of Dr. King.

The Black Power concept that had already begun to emerge while he was still alive, and it struck a responsive chord in the bosom of African Americans, if not publicly then privately. Nationalism was inextricably woven into Black Power. Dr. James Cone must be given credit for trying to incorporate a theology into this concept and thus keep the church relevant during this time.

The concept of Pan-Africanism embraced African people everywhere. Nothing new, of course. It has been said, "The more things change, the more they remain the same." And while the Black church was involved in African Liberation Day ceremonies and programs and Black church men and women were present at the historic African People's Congress in Gary, Indiana, in 1972 and in the late seventies and early eighties in the mass-based independent, radical, nationalist, activist organizations like the National Black United Front (NBUF), it wasn't until 1983 when the Rev. Jesse L. Jackson decided that he would make a run for the White House that the Black church stepped forward and become the dominant force. It was natural that the Black church formed the backbone of this venture. While many can take credit for Jackson's phenomenal success, without the Black church there would have been no run. No hits and no errors. Jackson's success sowed the seeds that would eventuate into a harvest for others.

A notable example was the election of David Dinkins as mayor of New York. Mr. Dinkins had not only the prior work of Jackson but also he has a united African American church with him. So even on the continent, when Nelson Mandela came home from prison, one of his first stops was at the home of a Black churchman, Bishop Desmond Tutu.

In fact, Black churchmen Tutu and Rev. Allan Boesak have been at the forefront of the struggle in South Africa.

Let me conclude with a quote from Bishop J. W. Hood, "The church having opened the way for the development of the black man, other means have followed, and still others will follow until his opportunities are equal to that of any other race . . . . The African church will then have accomplished its special work—not till then."

Notes

1. Yosef ben-Jochannan, *African Origins of the Major Western Religions* (New York: Alkebu-Lan Books, 1970). Also see the tract by Rev. Herbert Daughtry, "Was Jesus Black?" distributed by The House of the Lord Church, 415 Atlantic Avenue, Brooklyn, NY 11217.
2. W.E.B DuBois, "The Souls of Black Folk," in *Three Negro Classics* (New York: Avon Books, 1965), p.342.

3. Joseph R. Washington, Jr., *Black Religion* (Boston: Beacon Press, 1964).

4. E. Franklin Frazier, *The Negro Church in America* (New York: Schocken Books, 1963).

5. James Cone, *The Spirituals and the Blues* (New York: Seabury Press, 1972).

6. Nat Turner has been the object of criticism not only by whites but also by blacks who still depend upon whites to do their thinking. However, Gayraud Wilmore's assessment is the appropriate response:

> The most important thing to know about Nat Turner is that he is the prototype of an important group of slave preachers who had discovered a secret about the Judeo-Christian faith that white Christians had attempted to conceal from the slaves for more than two hundred years. Nat Turner, like others before him whose names are buried forever under the debris of the citadel of slavery, discovered that the God of the Bible demanded justice and that to know Him and His Son, Jesus Christ, was to be set free from every power on earth. Nat Turner discovered his manhood by unveiling the God who liberates. His fanatical attempt to authenticate that manhood in blood was the inevitable consequence of fanatical attempt of white men to deny it.

Gayraud S. Wilmore, *Black Religion and Black Radicalism* (Garden City, New York: Anchor Books, 1973), p. 89.

7. Wilmore, p. 100.

8. Ibid.

9. Ibid., p. 43.

10. Ibid., pp. 100-101.

11. John Hope Franklin, *From Slavery to Freedom* (New York: Random House), p. 309.

12. Herbert Daughtry, Sr., *Now Let Us Praise Black Preachers* (New York, The House of The Lord Church), February 12, 1977.

PART II

THEOLOGY OF BLACK LIBERATION

"My Lord, what a morning when the stars begin to fall,
you'll hear the trumpet sound, to wake the nation . . .
Looking to my God's right hand . . .
My Lord what a morning."

—African American Spiritual

Then sang Moses and the children of Israel this song unto
the LORD, and spake, saying, I will sing unto the LORD, for
he hath triumphed gloriously: the horse and his rider hath
he thrown into the sea. The LORD is my strength and song,
and he is become my salvation: he is my God, and I will
prepare him an habitation; my father's God, and I will exalt
him. The LORD is a man of war: the LORD is his name.

—Exodus 15:1-3

He hath shewed strength with his arm; he hath scattered
the proud in the imagination of their hearts. He hath put
down the mighty from their seats, and exalted them of low
degree. He hath filled the hungry with good things; and
the rich he hath sent empty away.

—Luke 1:51-53

Black people became Christians for intellectual, existential, and political reasons. Christianity is, as Friedreich Nietzsche has taught us and liberation theologians remind us, a religion especially fitted to the oppressed. It looks at the world from the perspective of those below. The African slaves' search for identity could find historical purpose in the exodus of Israel out of slavery and personal meaning in the bold identification of Jesus Christ with the lowly and downtrodden. Christianity also is first and foremost a theodicy, a triumphant account of good over evil. The intellectual life of the African slaves, in the United States— like that of all oppressed peoples—consisted primarily of reckoning with the dominant form of evil in their lives. The Christian emphasis on against-the-evidence hope for triumph over evil struck deep among many of them.

—Cornel West, *Prophesy Deliverance!*
Philadelphia: The Westminster Press,
182, p.35

A Theology of Black Liberation From a Black Perspective: The What, Who, and How

The "What" of Liberation

A theology of liberation derives validity from the situation of blackness in the United States of America.

The perception of reality, the cosmology, eschatology, teleology, and the frame of reference, growing out of the apparent innocence of this word "black," have created and perpetuated institutions, attitudes, values, and lifestyles that promote the well-being of white humanity and degrade black humanity.

The above is stated as a point of departure. It is inconceivable that anyone who has thought seriously on the race issue would offer any refutation. Even the President's Commission on Civil Disorders came to the conclusion that the ghettos of America were white-created and white-perpetuated, and that our nation was becoming two nations. This exceptional observation is rather revealing, for America, in the minds of black people, has always been two nations. The commission seems to be saying that the state of two nations exists because "we now recognize this to be the case." Thus, the commission unconsciously revealed that they were tainted with the prevailing disposition of treating blacks as nonexistent. Oh, Blacks were recognized as existing when they rioted. Watts is there, Bed-Stuy is there, because they went up in smoke. Otherwise, they would have been nonexistent to white society.

For those who answer, "But whites are exploited and dehumanized too," still there is a real, though often intangible entry into the society open to whites by virtue of their race, which is closed to blacks.

For those who do not acknowledge indirect or unconscious participation in the exploitative or oppressive structures, the words of Salley and Behm are most appropriate:

> Maintenance of the basic racial controls is now less dependent upon specific discriminatory decisions and acts. Such behavior has become so well institutionalized that the individual generally does not have to exercise a choice to operate in a racist manner. The rules and procedures of the large organizations have already pre-structured the choice. The individual only has to conform to the operating norms of the organization, and the institution will do the discriminating for him.[1]

Encircling this whiteness, validating it, sustaining it, permeating it, protecting it, justifying it is the white god of Christianity. If there is any doubt at all, one need but look at Christianity's hymnology, sermons, art, theologies, symbolisms, and rituals. Moreover, from a black perspective, white oppressive structures and Christianity have always been inextricably woven together.

In the book *Your God Is Too White*, the authors document the thinking of blacks relative to Christianity and social structures during three periods of American history. During slavery, they write,

> It is highly significant to note that any subsequent intellectual or psychological response of black people to the institution of slavery would by definition be a response to a 'Christianity' which was inextricably united with the oppressive forces of white dominance. Early in the black man's experience with Christianity the image developed in his intropsychic structure that Christianity is synonymous with whiteness which is synonymous with oppression."[2]

During the period of segregation, they write,

> The tragedy of the black experience during segregation was
> that blacks perceived Christianity as the chief support for
> the forces of racism that shaped these negative intro-psy-
> chic attitudes and social deprivations.[3]

And in the present "ghettoization", as they term it, they write,

> Christianity during ghettoization had only to submit qui-
> etly to the prevailing racist attitudes and practices which
> had now become an inseparable part of urban institutions....
> Because white 'Christians' had participated in and had sup-
> ported black subordination through American history, it
> was no longer necessary for the white church to openly
> espouse white domination.[4]

In the light of the foregoing, the disillusionment and disdain of Christianity by some blacks can be appreciated. The miracle is that
there are black Christians at all.

It is no wonder that there have always been no small number of
voices among us urging us to believe that we are the "elect," the
vanguard people, for we have borne or we have been the victims of
incalculable sufferings in the name of this God. Yet, we have been
faithful to Him and have sung His praises even in a strange land.
That, I might add, is more than the ancient Hebrews could do.
Liberation for blacks, then, would mean liberation from a white
God and his structures of exploitation and dehumanization.

At this point, secularization, using Cox's definition—"It is the
loosing of the world from religious and quasi-religious understand-
ings of itself, the dispelling of all closed world-views, the breaking
of all supernatural myths and sacred symbols"[5]—could be positive
in that it dethrones the old God and thus creates a vacuum into
which the true God could appear.

It is questionable, however, that any good will come of it. The
primary reason is that it is still the dominant white group defining a
situation from its perspective.

"Secularization has come." For Whom? "God has died in our
time, in our experience, in our history." Whose God? Whose time?
Whose experience? Whose history?

Into the vacuum they rushed more white analyses and answers. Having initially located God in the wrong place (in institutions and mores of western culture), they continued to play God, pontificating from their narrow experience and data. They expounded on the demise of God in the present and extrapolated the shape of His resurrection or reappearance in the future.

While outside, as usual, blacks, speaking from another perspective, were saying, *God lives! I saw him on the road to Birmingham, Alabama. I saw him in Washington, and not in the White House, but in Resurrection City. I saw him in the ghettos all across the country. I saw him in the rebellion at Attica Prison. And, I heard him in the wailing cries of babies bitten by rats. God lives!*

And as Dr. King used to say, "When the old prophet raised the question a long time ago, 'Is there a balm in Gilead? Is there a physician there?'" We took the question mark and straightened it into an exclamation point, and began to declare unto the world: "There *is* balm in Gilead! There *is* a physician there!"

The fact is, however, God never really died. Secularization never really came. Man is still incurably religious. As Martin E. Marty points out, man's religion often changes forms.[6] The old gods are yet alive in the land.

Liberation for blacks would also mean liberation from self-estrangement, self-hatred, and meaninglessness.

Who is prepared to determine how much of the above is due to demonic systems? It is indisputable that a negative self-image and destructive behavior patterns have invariably characterized cultural disintegration.

Dr. Martin Luther King used to say that to destroy a man's dignity, his somebodiness, was worse than killing him, for you have destroyed the essential quality that makes him what he is. He would go on to draw the analogy of clipping a bird's wings. It would be better to kill the bird than to pull off his wings. To chop his pinions is to snatch from him the very thing that makes him a bird. You have destroyed his "birdness." His potential for soaring the heavens, of ranging the horizons is gone. He hops and hobbles in a living death of meaninglessness.

Liberation encompasses more than emancipation from external restraints and internal estrangement. It includes a going from something *to* something; coming out of somewhere to get *to* somewhere.

For blacks, liberation from white systems and attitudes comprehends both liberation for an authentic personhood and purposefulness, grounded in a now possible commitment to the true God revealed in the real Jesus Christ and also the possibility of building new, just social structures.

The peculiarity of the black situation in the U.S.A. makes its liberation struggle unlike any other struggle. It is not a march to a new land. It is not a carving up of a piece of this land, although both positions had and still have advocates. At some point in the future either may prove to be the only solution.

It is not even necessarily the physical death of those who are the oppressors. It is, rather, the reform in some instances and the replacement in others of the institutions of the social order, so that they might be responsive to human needs and aspirations—so minimal and yet so monumental.

Now, to bring about radical rearrangement, any action might be feasible. Biblically, God has been generous in His use of all kinds of men and all kinds of means to usher in a new order.

We are fortunate in the U.S.A. that avenues are open that, if utilized, preclude the need for violent confrontation. To the external credit of the founding fathers, they provided for redress of grievances. "The congress shall make no laws abridging the right of the people to petition their government," the noble document reads. It is doubtful, however, that the founding fathers had blacks in mind in preparation of the document, since they declared that a black was 3/5 of a man. Chief Justice Taney so understood the constitution, he states in the Dred Scott Decision, "Black folks have no rights white folks were bound to respect."

One might ask, how could an intelligent person prepare documents identifying independence with God's will while holding other human beings slaves? It is important for us to ask that question today, for the way the founding fathers answered it pushed the nation further along the path of dualism and further fertilized the soil for continued animosity and hardened the illusions of existence. To maintain a psychological balance, slave-holding writers of independence had to negate the black "other."

Really though, in fairness to the founding fathers, they accepted the myth that had existed since the beginning of the slave traffic, for the founding fathers' fathers had to settle the question relative to the rape of Africa: How can so-called Christian people re-create and sustain a system of slavery? Again, the "other," in this case Africans, were not human beings but non-humans, sub-humans, and the children of the founding fathers continued the process of negation.

"To petition their government" covers a multitude of possible actions. If the constitutional means are not utilized, the stage is then set for violent confrontation.

I remember writing, at the time that black power was provoking national consternation,

> Stokely Carmichael is not the problem. The paradox of his presence is that he is good for America. He represents the last appeal of non-violent change. The next turn will be in a more organized and violent direction.

Since then we've had riots and urban unrest. We have seen the emergence of the Black Panther Party and the Black Liberation Army. Who knows what comes next.

Liberation for blacks would mean liberation for whites too. The mentality that needs a nigger, i.e. that predicates an existence upon the nonexistence of another, is abnormal. Liberation for blacks would mean salvation for whites.

Booker T. Washington used to say, "You can't keep a man in a ditch without staying there with him."

Similarly Salley and Behm argued,

> The white man can only be free of his racism as he is forced to view blacks (using definitions of blacks and being confronted by blacks) as human, political and economic equals. Only when this becomes a reality will there be a demise of the subtleties of racism as manifested by white paternalism, ignorance and fear.[7]

There is another dimension to this liberation. Once blacks and whites crush the illusion by which both have defined their existence, other illusions will explode too; illusions of power and politics; of poverty and prosperity; illusions of flag and religion.

The "Who" of Liberation

Who is the "who" of liberation? The "who" of liberation is always God. God wills liberation.

> The Spirit of the Lord is upon me, because he has anointed me to preach good news to the poor. He has sent me to proclaim release to the captives and recovering of sight to the blind, to set at liberty those who are oppressed, to proclaim the acceptable year of the Lord. (see Luke 4:18-19)

But to say that God wills liberation does not mean that all methods employed to obtain liberation are anchored in God. The end does not justify all means. The method employed by God at one point in history may be inappropriate at another time. A severe test of faith comes when we are called on to obey God when He seems to contradict his own policy and jeopardize his own purpose. God, however, liberates through human channels. So the question is, "Who is God using in his liberation activities?"

Now we need not think that God is confined to use only those who profess to follow Him. No one would argue with the poet, "He that would be free must himself strike the first blow." But does that mean he not only strikes the first blow, but all the blows?

"We wish to plead our own cause, for too long others have pleaded for us."[8]

But does that mean that others cannot importune too? Even though, through the accident of birth, they are members of the race or class to be challenged?

To raise this question is to hear the cries "Black Power!" "Missionary go home." "Whitey get out of our community!" it is to ask, "What is the role of whites?"

The question has precipitated a plethora of "What to Do" kits, from Nathan Wright's *Black Power and Urban Unrest* to James Forman's *Black Manifesto*. Innumerable blacks have spent their time and energy addressing themselves to that question. The situation, however, has not changed in any appreciable degree. Plainly then, more instruction and programs are not the answer. The question itself is loaded with the potential to perpetuate the problem, for it implies a master-slave stance. The implication is that whites have so much to give—"What do you poor people want from us?"

Those who hasten in with a list of "What to Do" kits manifest what Richard Wright calls "a frog perspective," always looking up to whites.

It seems to me that James Cone is right. Whites would have to stop being white and become black: And those who wish to join us in the divine work must be willing to lose their white identity—indeed destroy it.[9] He clarifies what is meant by blackness.

> First, blackness is a physiological trait. It refers to a particular black-skinned people in America who have been victims of white racist brutality . . . Secondly, blackness is the ontological symbol for all people who participate in the liberation of man from oppression.[10]

It is as an ontological symbol that I employ the term here. As Cone rightly points out, it includes all oppressed, dehumanized humanity.

The initial step in doing something for the oppressed is to become like them; to take their suffering and dehumanization as one's very own. God, Himself, has shown us the way. He took upon Himself the corruption of human nature. He became man.

Any white who takes on blackness will have little difficulty knowing what he ought to do. The first question for whites then is, "How can I be black?" "How can I be?" That is the question; Not the question of doing, but of being: "What is my identity in these pressing times?"

There are two considerations relative to white conversion to blackness that cannot be overstated. It would enhance the credibility of mission work in other parts of the world. The day of mission is not ended. It can never be ended for two reasons. It is God's work *and* (as Dr. Long pointed out the other evening),[11] God's priority.

Mission does not rest with the whims of men, but with the wishes of God. Emilio Castro, Director of the Commission on World Mission and Evangelism, said it well: "End of a missionary era, yes. But the end of mission, never. Because the God in whom we believe is a missionary God."

Mission grows out of an imperative brought on by an encounter with Jesus the Christ. Let me say here that the question whether or not the Gospel should be preached to other religions or ideologies seems to miss the point. One can only be what he is. To say to a person who has met the Lord in the depth of his being, "Be still, be quiet" is comparable to saying to light, "Do not shine." In our church we sing a song, "I said I wasn't gonna' tell nobody, but I couldn't keep it to myself—What the Lord has done for me." Whoever has found peace and purpose in our confused, troubled, and chaotic world has an obligation to share it. Everyone ought to have the right to decide whether or not to accept it. How the reflection is made is open to question, but that is not the same as saying, Let there be no reflection.

It would seem to me that the shift in these present times would take three directions. First, support, in whatever form it is requested, for the indigenous missions (and we have heard throughout this conference they seem to be doing very well).

Second, an abdication of the dominant white role, here and abroad. You've been at it a long time. Step aside.

Third, make the six-continent approach an immediate reality. Open wide the gates. Let the so-called third world missionaries come in—waves and waves of them, and not just a few scholars —and invest the same ingenuity, finance, time, and energy in this "Back across the ocean approach" as was invested in those happy days of yore when the "dark" land of Africa beckoned you (or at least so you thought).

Now, if you would send out an urgent Macedonian call, Come to the asphalt jungle and the canyons of steel, it just might be that the West might be won.

Then, in terms of the conversion of whiteness to blackness, it would irrevocably commit whites to the struggle for justice. The eagerness to quit on programs and noble causes when there are no quick harvests, or when there is stiff opposition from a powerful majority would disappear (it is hoped). Having assumed the humiliation of blackness, whites would then be committed even though it meant the cross.

Whatever whites do or refuse to do is not the paramount problem for the oppressed. Such people must, somehow, come by the wherewithal to free themselves. Liberation can never be given by others. It must be taken by the oppressed themselves. "You can't be free if somebody lets you be free!"[12]

Now if there is a concomitant strategy for spiritual change while one is about the business of reordering social structures, or if there is a tactic for social change while spiritual change is sought, then true liberation might be possible. The ideal strategy would merge what we have come to call spiritual and social action, always cognizant that whatever is done must produce an interior change. Otherwise we have missed the mark.

This brings us to the Gospel of Jesus Christ. It is my firm conviction, from subjective and objective experience, that the Gospel of Jesus Christ, divested of its choking cultural accessories, exercises the most potent force to effect meaningful change. The scripture leaves no doubt on this point. "The gospel is the power of God unto salvation (Romans 1:16 [RSV])." "If the Son shall make you free, you shall be free indeed (John 8:36 [RSV])."

He who encounters Christ will become a new creation or person. His desires, his value system, his thought processes, his character and attitudes will experience a thorough redoing. Inevitably, God's self-disclosure produces a new being. As he wrestles with the almighty, Jacob, a haunted, deceptive, disintegrated self becomes Israel, a prince of God; and after encountering Christ in the dust, Saul, a troubled, destructive man, becomes Paul, a positive, God-possessed personality.

The new state of being elicits the question, unconsciously or consciously, How shall the new self be expressed in the social order? Shall it be against culture, of culture, above culture, culture in paradox, or transformer of culture?[13]

The Pentecostal movement, the charismatic movement, that is sweeping the country, invokes this question. Is it simply another escapism, a kind of infantile womb search? How shall the new self express its meaning in the social order? Shall it go outward, and if so, in which direction? Converting others to Jesus without regard to social structures, or converting to Christianity with little or no concern for personal salvation, or both? Changes for individuals and/or institutions? So much will depend on how the new self becomes new in the first place. Obviously He who brought the light will exercise compelling influence. The priorities and emphasis of the church, where He works out his new lifestyle and the cultural arrangements will have significant influence.

In America the Pentecostal movement adheres to the racial and class patterns of the larger society. In the beginning it was not so. At 312 Azuza Street, Los Angeles, California, the place where the real explosion occurred, there were no race or class lines. There was such intense seeking after God and such extraordinary experiences that the color and bank book questions were relegated to oblivion.

Had this continued and spilled out into the larger society, it might have revolutionized American society, but, alas, in a few years it had fallen into race and class grooves.

Today the black Pentecostal church in the U.S.A. is indistinguishable from its conservative, otherworldly, pietistic counterpart. In other countries Pentecostalism assumes a different shape.

In Russia, Pentecostals have no quarrel with communism or with the essentials of the social political system, although they have opposed the government ban on Sunday schools and open-air meetings. Their charge is that the Russian government has not really been communist. They insist that Russia is not really constitutional in the broader sense of that term, because the basic legal and political structures of Russian society do not reflect the thinking of Lenin and Marx. To Brezhnev, for example, they cite tests from the writings of Lenin and Marx that decry the Czar's persecution of religious minorities and promise that when the communist state comes, every citizen will enjoy complete freedom, not only to believe what he wants but also to propagate his faith. Where, then, is religious freedom in our communist state? they ask.

In Scandinavia, it is compulsory to learn the history of trade unions in Pentecostal bible schools. Norwegian Pentecostals were strongly opposed to American involvement in the war in Vietnam and supported diplomatic ties between their government and that of North Vietnam.

And finally, Manual De Mello, a Pentecostal pastor in Brazil whose followers number in the millions, gave his reason for joining the World Council of Churches. He said that he wanted to teach the members of the council how to worship. "They were like a body of dry bones." But, he wanted to learn also the sociological techniques he thought they knew. "What good does it do," he asks, "to convert a million people if at the same time the devil unconverts ten million through hunger, disease, and military dictatorship." These sort of things cannot be overcome by holding wonderful religious services, but by organizing one's forces and joining with others who have similar interests. We must join now (and this shows De Mello's liberalism) with other Protestants and even with Roman Catholics to help each other.[14]

In Africa, the indigenous or independent church movement, which Dr. David Barrett, in a study made in 1967, estimated that there were some five thousand distinct ecclesiastical and religious bodies in thirty-four African nations, with a total of almost seven million nominal adherents drawn predominantly from two hundred and ninety different tribes in all parts of the continent, and they take on rich and varied posture in their worship, morality, and mission, as Dr. John Mbiti has already stated.

There seems to be a principle that, with proper cultivation, if there is no negative intervention, we will attempt to duplicate in the social order what we have accepted and lived with first in the mental or spiritual order.

Implied in the Gospel is the proposition that if a man is really set free spiritually, so that he comes to see himself as a child of God with cosmic citizenship and divine rights, he will not need Big Daddies and white benefactors to change his social system. He will do it himself. He might ask for assistance, but the request will be put on his own terms. Alive with a new sense of his somebodiness, he will not submit to injustice and exploitation.

He will have to fight, struggle, work for structural change, so that what he is inside can live with the world outside. Where, for whatever reason he feels he has to resign himself to an unjust situation, he has a rationale for his action. He does it by choice, not by compulsion.

The profoundly significant point is that the Gospel of Jesus Christ has the potential to dispose a person to deal creatively with his situation. If change is what is needed, whether internal or external, he will so engage himself in the appropriate action. Whatever the situation requires, the dynamics of the Gospel or the encounter with Christ can prove sufficient for the occasion.

Moreover, he will not permit demonic systems to dehumanize anyone without a challenge from him....even though he himself may not be directly affected. Jesus' action in the temple is our example. He did not act to defend or promote his own interest. It was on behalf of others.

In addition, a new definition of self forces the exploiter to redefine himself. Proper evaluation of one's worth circumscribes the actions of the oppressor. Self-awareness sets limits upon the racist. James Cone writes, "When oppressed people come to know who they are, they will not tolerate oppression."[15]

Who cooperates, who does the mission work or the evangelizing or the liberating cannot be decided in advance. Disqualification of a potential ally on the basis of race or class is immature and raises questions relative to the seriousness of one's desire for liberation. At a given point, separation might be useful. At still another, wisdom might dictate partial involvement. There are times when complete cooperation would be viable.

It may serve a provisional purpose in some situations for a missionary to go home, but all who profess to follow Jesus entertain the hope that the day when missionaries will be welcome — at least among those who profess the same God — is close at hand. The challenge always before the disciples of Jesus is that "they might be one." Jesus said, "By this shall all men know that you are my disciples, if you have love, one for another...."[16]

Interpreting Colossians 3:11-15, Colin Williams wrote:
Here there can not be Greek and Jew (the dividing wall of nation and race), circumcised and uncircumcised (the barriers of religiousness), barbarian or scythian (the clash of cultures) slaves, free man (the hostilities or class), but Christ is all in all.[17]

In a world fragmented and broken by race and color and class and culture and all sorts of things, to have a visible family of humanity, from all the peoples of the earth, bound together by a common loyalty to Jesus the Christ would exert an irresistible attraction and more importantly, would expand the personality of all as each finds himself in the other.

The "How" of Liberation

Now the "How" of liberation can be classified into four categories as I observe them in Holy Writ.

1. *Liberation that comes as a result of special events or developments that cause the oppressor to change his mind, with-*

out action from the enslaved.

Pharaoh changes his mind after a series of catastrophes, culminating in the death of the boy babies in Egypt by the destroying angel (Exodus 12:30, 31). The slaves left Egypt without firing a shot or raising a sword. It may not be too far-fetched to speculate that the death of the Egyptian babies was a tactic of the liberator. After all, the destruction of the man child had been part of Egypt's political agenda for years. [See also the story of Jehoshaphat (II Chronicles 20) and of Hezekiah (II Chronicles 32:1-22)].

2. *Liberation by human agents chosen by God, other than the oppressed.*

The Israelites' liberation from Babylonian captivity by Cyrus, a heathen, or at least one who did not believe in the God of Israel. Significantly, God calls him "my anointed" (Isaiah 45:1). While Israel was liberated through the intervention of others, still it was Nehemiah who built the walls with a sword at his side (Nehemiah 4:17, 18).

3. *Liberation by the oppressed themselves. See the story of Gideon (Judges 7).*

4. *Liberation by a coalition of the oppressed with others.*

When we come to Jesus we are in the presence of a new method and style of liberation. Jesus does not gather people to launch a physical assault upon the system, although He is very physical in the temple. He does not organize any social strategy to change social situations. He had no political platform.

Now, whether this was because Jesus knew that any traditional liberation activity would be futile at that time; or that He knew that once He changed men's thinking about themselves, they would know what had to be done, since all revolution begins in the mind; or, that He was only concerned with building a spiritual kingdom and therefore set the pattern that was to be the approach in every age; or that it was a combination of the last two.

To wit, He was building a spiritual kingdom with new values and lifestyles, and once men embraced this kingdom they would move to change society. Whatever the reasons, Jesus was no violent liberator, nor was he an advocate of the same.

It does not strain credulity too much to conjecture that a part of the agony in the Garden of Gethsemane—indeed, throughout His ministry—had to do with whether he would go peaceably to the cross, or put up an armed struggle. For angels of all kinds, celestial and terrestrial, were at His command (John 18:36). Certainly a great number of the throngs who followed Him would have done battle for Him, as evidenced by Peter who chopped off the guard's ear. Also, Jesus knew that Peter had a sword. Even if He had been just an ordinary soul, He would have observed the weapon. But right up to his apprehension, he let Peter keep his saber. Why? Was it because He was still wrestling with the methodology of the Kingdom? In any event he went without resistance, and the cross stands forever as a symbol of God's unfathomable self-giving.

With this act did Jesus mean that He would not establish His kingdom upon violence, for this is the way of the world, and all these kingdoms perpetuate injustice and come to naught?

Did He leave open the question of violence, or the exercise of power and resources on behalf of the oppressed? Again, Jesus in the temple is our model. He vents his fury against an exploitative system on behalf of others, and at the same time teaches, "Turn the other cheek."

And finally, what is meant by his return in power and great glory (Matthew 24:27-31.)? A supernatural breaking into history from beyond? Or rather the coming to power, spiritually and naturally, of his disciples through whom he cuts the wicked asunder and thereby ushers in the millennium ... since God has always come in human form or done his work through human instrumentality.

When one ponders the technological miracles that raise the prospects of developing and utilizing the universe so that not only is longevity possible but also a quality of life unknown heretofore, a golden age does not seem so incredible. If the above bears any semblance of truth, did the disciples of Jesus so understand his return?

But does all this mean that Jesus was not a revolutionary? I would say He was, and I would go further and say that He was more revolutionary than those who have borne the appellation. He stands, as it were, on the other side of revolutionaries. When they have done their work, or when He works with them to do their work, He then challenges them to be revolutionized. What do I mean?

Carl Braaten calls attention to eight characteristics of Jesus's approach that show the revolutionary nature of his ministry. If you would, at certain points, you can say, Where do I stand? Ordinarily, in my church, we say "Amen!"

1. *The demand for total change.* There is a complete break with the old order. You must be born anew. Old loyalties must be sundered. Values must no longer be defined by the system. Treasures or values must be eschatological, beyond the contamination of history.

2. *The concept to the demonic.* The visible political structures, powers, and principalities are but the manifestation of a demonic principle that is operative in the spirit, and they must be vanquished.

3. *The sign of the times.* The existing realities are not all. They point to the ultimate occurances from the future.

4. *The urgency of the moment.* The coming new order calls for thorough conversion now. You cannot wait to choose sides. The kingdom is at hand. You are with it or against it.

5. *The unconditional surrender to service.* A revolutionary idea indeed. He that is greatest must be the servant of all.

6. *The proletarian principle.* It is a revolution that gathers into the kingdom the dispossessed. It does not exclude the rich and powerful. It requires them to cease dependency on these idols, to give them away or to bring them into the service of the kingdom.

7. *The reversal of rules.* The last shall be first and the first last (Mark 10:30). The outs shall be called in, and the ins shall be thrown out. Those who are exalted are under judgement (Luke

16:16). What it means to be first or to win is radically altered. In a revolution the oppressed must confuse or change the symbols of the oppressor.

8. *The birth pangs of a glorious future.* When the demonic threatens engulfment, rejoice, for God standeth watch above his own. Celebrate hard times for the hour of victory is near and speeding fast.[18]

How shall we reconcile the violent liberation activities of God in the Old Testament with the apparent nonviolent methods of Jesus in the New Testament?

How shall we resolve the liberation for physical space accomplished for a people with national identity over against the nonphysical space, metaphysical peoplehood, kingdom of the Spirit liberation?

Can Moses and Jesus walk together? Are they contradictory or complementary? Is there a dialectical handle for which we must always be reaching?

One approach would be to project the Old Testament violence into the future, plant the seeds of the Gospel securing a spiritual radicalization of self, and leave open the means to be employed for liberation in the present. Thus, the hope of an eschatological redemption — whether arising out of history or coming from beyond history or from above history — can be held while existential struggle continues with different people utilizing different means in different places at different times.

Not much more can be said. To ask for more is to ask for what the scripture cannot give.

Our faith is not a static, inflexible straight jacket, but a dynamic interaction with the person, Jesus the Christ. Out of the relationship comes guidance in every situation. He guides into all truth.

> There is no firm foothold in history, to each day the people of God have to touch down in a new situation of events through which God is free to act on the spur of the moment.[19]

The God of our faith, who is the God of the oppressed, is the God who keeps Himself free to act. He does not allow Himself to be captured in the traditions and methodologies of yesterday. Even in our finiteness we can perceive the wisdom of this.

Man is an inveterate idolizer of his achievements and experiences. He expects the God of his father to live in the shape and structures in which his father knew Him. This propensity often constrains God to war against the very forms and fashions in which He once appeared and acted.

The God of our faith exercises his freedom to act and to use whomever and whatever He wills, where ever, when ever and however He wills. And because God is free, this freedom is potentially ours.

Notes

1. Columbus Salley and Ronald Behm, *Your God Is Too White* (Downers Grove, IL: Intervarsity Press, 1970), p. 43.
2. Ibid., p. 22.
3. Ibid., p. 37.
4. Ibid., p. 44.
5. Harvey Cox, *The Secular City* (New York: Macmillan Co., 1966), p. 2.
6. Martin E. Marty, *Search for a Usable Future* (New York: Harper & Row, 1969).
7. Salley and Behm, p. 72.
8. Editorial, in *Freedom Journal*, March 16, 1827.
9. James Cone, *Black Theology, Black Liberation* (Philadelphia and New York: J.B. Lippincott Co., 1970), p. 120.
10. Ibid., p. 37.
11. Dr. Charles H. Long, Jr. was the newly appointed Executive Secretary for t he United States of the World Council of Churches in 1974.
12. New York subway graffiti.
13. Richard Niebuhr, *Christ and Culture* (New York: Harper & Brothers, 1951).
14. H. Hollenweger, *Pentecostalism* - Third World, Dialog.
15. Ibid.
16. Ibid.
17. Colin Williams, *Where in the World* (New York: National Council of Church, 475 Riverside Drive, 1963), p. 28.
18. Carl Braaten, *Christ and Counter Christ* (Philadelphia: Fortress Press, 1972), pp. 111-113.
19. Ibid.

CHAPTER TWO

PART I
THREAT FROM THE NEW RIGHT

PART II
HISTORY OF RACISM OR
COLOR PREJUDICE

THREAT FROM THE NEW RIGHT—
TRACING THE HISTORY
OF AN OLD WRONG

The challenge of this conference, "In Defense of the Constitution, a Threat from the New Right" (Charleston, WV, May 7-8, 1982) should be placed in a historical context. Therefore, I want to speak on "Threat from the New Right—Tracing the History of an Old Wrong." I do want to beg your indulgence as I use racism as my point of departure. My intention here is not to focus solely on the injustice to which Black people have been the constant victims. Nevertheless, I am firm in the conviction that a nation is as strong as its weakest link, or more appropriate for this occasion, justice or the constitution can only be viewed with respect if it safeguards the rights of its most defenseless citizens. When the weak citizen is denied his right, to that extent everyone's rights are jeopardized. For one season, the abrogation of the rights of the powerless may redound to the benefit of the powerful, but eventually the law of universal justice will even the score.

The way people are treated —and the same could be said for Chicanos, Native Americans, Latinos, Asians, etc.,—is a commentary upon American society and more specifically upon its legal system.

Racism—Past and Present
Racism in American society is a historic as well as a contemporary reality. By racism I mean that which promotes one people at the expense of another people. I want to classify racism in three categories:

1. sadistic racism;
2. sophisticated racism, and
3. simple racism .

Sadistic racism is of a blatant, brutal nature. It boldly declares its intent. It has no love for Black people and says so unequivocally. It employs whatever it can to subjugate Black people. This is exemplified by the KKK.

Sophisticated racism is the more subtle kind of racism. In this category are the profit-seekers who benefit from racism. Often times they show themselves friendly to Black people and will in fact give assistance to Blacks. Some of the so-called liberals are found in this category.

Simple racism is the category of the majority of people. They go along with the program. They are "nice" people. They would not think of themselves as racist or even enjoying the fruits of racism. What they cannot understand—or refuse to understand—is that the existing social structures are rooted in the subjugation and exploitation of Black people, and, therefore, to simply go along with the program is a form of racism.

There is an attitude toward racism that is the opposite of the aforementioned three categories; "shatterers" of racism. This category of people understand the sadistic and sophisticated character of racism and courageously try to swat it out of existence. This group is a small minority, but it has always existed. This group particularly needs to be supported now. The New Right has fixed its cannon upon them.

A piece of history from which we can learn is that of Nazi Germany. The three categories that I have identified with respect to racism were evident in Germany with regards to anti-Semitism. There were the sadistic anti-Semites. i.e., the Nazis who conceived the most inhumane programs of death and torture for Jews; the sophisticated anti-Semites, i.e., who profited from the genocide; and the simple anti-Semites, i.e., the majority of Germans who went along with the program for various reasons.

We should understand that the development of racism derived from the raping and ravishing of Africa, from slavery, and from colonialism. It was an attempt to justify sadistic behavior.

Capitalism and Slavery

The slave system was one of the major foundations upon which American economy rested. Some people argue that it was the shift in the economic system, towards industrialization, that detracted from the importance of slavery and really brought on the Civil War. Even with the termination of this system, Blacks were not provided with the material means to enable them to adjust to the new state of things. In this we see racism at work. It was surely obvious that unless there was substantial assistance to the former slaves, they would still be at the mercy of racism.

Further still, even when the U.S.A. was moving from an agricultural to an industrial society, Blacks were not brought into the system; instead, laborers were brought in from Europe and even from Asia. Keep in mind, these immigrants were given all kinds of assistance (land grants, subsidies, training assistance, machinery, etc.), and these are the same people who a few years later, and their children still later, would be urging Black people to pull themselves up by their own bootstraps and deny that they themselves were the beneficiaries of the fruits of racism. Today the economic system is still working against Black people, but now the unfairness of the economic system is also venting its brutalities upon whites.

Political

All forms of racism were manifested in the political system. Black people have been excluded from the political process for most of American history. What America claimed to have fought for, no taxation without representation, was not extended to Blacks. Recall Thomas Jefferson's lofty words, "We hold these truths to be self-evident, that all people are created equal and are endowed by their creator with certain inalienable rights. Among these, life, liberty, and the pursuit of happiness." Significantly, Thomas Jefferson changed the last word, originally it had been "property". These lofty sentiments were not extended to Black people.

But a particular development occurred. Black people did not count; they did not exist as far as many white people were concerned. But some white people said, Oh, yes, they exist. We have them on our plantations and we want them counted. But, you cannot count them, other White people said, because they are your slaves. Yes they exist but they belong to you. Alright, they said, let us compromise, we will count them as 3/5 of men. So today, right there in the Constitution, it is recorded:

> Representatives and direct taxes shall be apportioned among the several states which may be included within this Union, according to their respective numbers, which shall be determined by adding to the whole number of free persons, including those bound to service for a term of years, and excluding Indians not taxed, 3/5 of all other persons.

Note the emasculation. Blacks exist, but they are not as much as other people, and their worth must be determined by other, more advanced human beings—slave holders and their friends.

Sadistic, sophisticated, and simple racists all agreed on the compromise. There were but a few "shatterers" of racism who fought against the compromise, John Brown being one. It is no wonder, then, that Chief Justice Tanney ruled in the Dred Scott case essentially that "Black people had no rights White people where bound to respect."

Let us not be deceived by those who were supposed to be "shatterers" of racism, for example Abraham Lincoln. Old Abe is held forth as the model of humanitarianism and lover of Black folks and all that. But the record gives us a different Lincoln, one who clearly wavered in his decision to issue the Emancipation Proclamation. Lincoln said to one lobbying delegation that he could not free slaves under the Constitution, because it could not be enforced in the rebel states. When it was finally issued on September 22, 1863, the Emancipation Proclamation said:

> All persons held as slaves within any state, or designated part of the state, the people whereof shall be in rebellion against the United States, shall be then, hence forward and forever free.

Lincoln made the termination of slavery depend upon the decision of the rebellious slave-holding states. If they did not come back into the Union by a certain time, their slaves would be freed. Lincoln's threat stated clearly that the penalty for not staying within the Union would be the freeing of their slaves. If the slave states had come back into the Union, it is possible that Blacks would still be in slavery. Eight hundred thousand slaves were still held in bondage in those states "whereof the people were not in rebellion against the Union." Right here in West Virginia slaves were not freed. Forty-eight counties of Virginia now constitute West Virginia, which was then not in rebellion against the Union. And let us not forget that it was quite awhile before Lincoln would use Black soldiers, in spite of Frederick Douglass' importunities, and even when slaves escaped to the Union lines they were not allowed to fight and in some instances were sent back.

The last paragraph of the Proclamation is revealing: "sincerely believed to be an act of justice arranged by the constitution." It was a military necessity. "Justice" and "Constitution," are wonderful ideals; but in reality it is a "military necessity."

In July 1861, General Winfield Scott wrote Brigade General McDonell in the name of Lincoln that he should allow owners of slaves to search out runaway slaves beyond Union lines in Virginia. It is interesting to note that there were some generals who were going further than Lincoln was prepared to go. In 1861, General John C. Fremont proclaimed freedom for the runaway slaves in Missouri; Lincoln modified the act. In 1862, General David Hunter proclaimed freedom for slaves in Georgia, South Carolina, and Florida.

Lincoln really wanted to get rid of Blacks. Colonization was really at the heart and in the heart of Lincoln. He hoped that there could be a gradual emancipation with compensation and then colonization. In August 1862, he convened a meeting with prominent Negroes to urge them to accept his plan. There were not many takers. The idea of emigration was not new. Innumerable Blacks not only argued in favor of it, but undertook to make it a reality. But my guess is, Blacks did not like Whites, even a president, telling them that they should leave the country.

It is not my intention to discredit Lincoln, but I am trying to show how deep and sophisticated American racism is, how it works in individuals and institutions, and we must recognize this if we are to understand the New Right and defeat it.

After the Civil War, it seemed that at last America would be an open society. Black people would be recognized as human beings.

The shatterers of racism were in the driver's seat. Representative Thaddeus Stevens and Charles Sumner were leading the way. There were attempts to redress inequalities in the Constitution. The 13th Amendment, adopted in 1865, ended slavery; the 14th Amendment, adopted in 1868, conferred citizenship; and the 15th Amendment, adopted in 1870, extended enfranchisement.

On March 2, 1867, Congress legislated that the former slave states should have conventions, and all male citizens were entitled to participate. (Notice here at this time women were treated less than human, and I might add that one of the foremost protagonists for Women's Rights was Frederick Douglass. It wasn't until 1920, when the 19th Amendment was adopted, that women were given suffrage.)

It should be pointed out here that, as John Hope Franklin observed, the state constitutions drawn up in 1867 and 1868 were the most progressive the South has ever known. Most of them abolished property qualifications for voting and holding office; some of them abolished imprisonment for debt. All of them abolished slavery, and several sought to eliminate race distinctions in the possession or inheritance of property.[1]

Between 1869 and 1880, Black people could boast sixteen members in the Congress of the United States, and of that number two were Senators. Today, we have 18 Representatives and no Senators.

The Freedman's Bureau, of which W.E.B. DuBois spoke so highly, was trying to assist the newly freed slaves. In 1866, Congress passed civil rights legislation over the veto of President Andrew Johnson, and in 1875 there was more civil rights legislation. But racism was not dead yet. Sadistic racists continued to employ the most vicious practices to intimidate Black people.

John Hope Franklin said it well: "as surely as the struggle between 1861 and 1865 was the civil war, so was the conflict from 1865 to 1877, with as much bitterness of hatred, but less bloodshed."[2] I would only add, less white blood but more black blood.

Secret societies grew and spread when it became apparent to Southerners that their control was to be broken by Radical Reconstruction. For ten years after 1867 there flourished the Knights of the White Camelia, the Constitutional Union Guards, the Pale Faces, the White Brotherhood, the Council of Safety, the '76 Association, and the Knights of the Ku Klux Klan. Among the numerous local organizations were the White League of Louisiana, the White Line of Mississippi, and the Rifle Clubs of South Carolina. White Southerners expected to do by extralegal or blatantly illegal means what had not been allowed by law: to exercise absolute control over the Negro, drive him and his fellows from power, and establish "white supremacy." Radical Reconstruction was to be ended at all costs, and the tactics of terrorist groups were the first step of Southern leaders toward achieving this goal.[3]

Significantly, beginning in Tennessee in 1870, every Southern state adopted laws against intermarriage. Five years later, Tennessee adopted the first "Jim Crow" law and the rest of the South quickly fell in line.

Then along came Rutherford B. Hayes. He wanted to become president, and to achieve that objective he was prepared to do anything. He made a deal with former slave holders; he would pull out the Federal troops, give money for development and greater representation in Washington for their support. In essence, he would restore the former slave masters to power in the South, and Black people would thus be returned to subjugation.

By the latter part of the 1870s, the Congress had turned against blacks. In 1878, the use of armed force to ensure fair election was forbidden. In 1894, the appropriations for Special Federal Marshals and Supervisors of Election were terminated. In 1898, the last disabilities laid on rebellious Southerners were removed in a final amnesty.

The Supreme Court, in spite of the Constitution, found a way to drive Blacks away from the temple of legal and human rights. In 1875, the Supreme Court overturned the Civil Rights Act of 1866, disregarded the legislation of 1870, which were enactments to stop KKK-type vigilantism. The court ruled in favor of defendants who were indicted for preventing blacks from voting. In the *United States v. Reese*, the court ruled that the statute covered more offenses than were punishable under the 15th Amendment. In the *United States v. Cruikshank*, the court ruled that the 15th Amendment guaranteed citizens not the right to vote, but only the right not to be discriminated against by states because of race, color, or previous conditions of servitude. In 1883, the court outlawed the Civil Rights Laws of 1875.

1890—*Plessy v. Ferguson*

By 1898, with the *Plessy v. Ferguson* decision, where the court ruled that there could be such a thing as separate and equal, all the noble efforts of the shatterers of racism had come to naught. So much for the Supreme Court and the defense of our constitutional rights. Men who have special interest, whose profession it is to deal with words, are like iron smiths, they can shape them any way they want to and when they have the power to enforce their will, their laws—right or wrong—become the law of the land. What is clear to some people: Words on paper mean absolutely nothing. To whom, then, shall we entrust the defense of the Constitution? To the courts? The Congresses? The presidents? All of them at one time or another have proven to be our enemy, and the enemies of the Constitution.

Sadistic racism coupled with sophisticated racism, with the support of simple racism, succeeded in beating back the shatterers of racism, trampling upon the recently enacted ideals of the Constitution and destroying the great work of radical reconstruction. There are striking similarities between that time and our own, which requires more time than I can give it in this presentation.

1898—1954

When the new century began there was nothing new about the treatment of black people; 214 lynchings occurred in the first two years. When the First World War broke out, Woodrow Wilson, like Thomas Jefferson before him, had lofty words of freedom, liberty, and democracy. He wanted to make the world safe for democracy —democracy for everyone but Black Americans.

Throughout the twenties, thirties, forties, and on into the fifties —in spite of the Constitution—disenfranchisement, economic exclusion, and social ostracism were the common lot of Black people in most states. This state of affairs carried the sanction of Law. "Separate but equal" was how the Supreme Court interpreted the Constitution, which came to mean separate but unequal. Everybody knew it, and most everybody accepted it. While Roosevelt was pulling America out of its depression in the thirties with a "New Deal" which for Blacks was a better deal but not a fair deal.

During the forties, A. Phillip Randolph, then president of the Brotherhood of Sleeping Car Porters, had to threaten a march on Washington to force President Roosevelt to pass a Fair Employment Practice Act. We rode with Teddy Roosevelt and his rough riders at the turn of the century. We died fighting Germans in the First World War. We went off to faraway places to fight Germans again, and Japanese, and Italians during the Second World War in the forties. During the fifties we went to fight Koreans in Korea, and we went to Vietnam to fight the Vietnamese in the sixties. It seems that every nationality has fought against the U.S.A., but African . . . Black people. But after all this loyalty, valor, scars, and death, we were still outside the blessing of the Constitution, and today our predicament is as precarious as it has ever been.

With the Supreme Court ruling in *Brown vs. the Board of Education* (1954), light began once more to penetrate the gloom of racism. Tragically, the court put in a few words which were really unnecessary: "with all deliberate speed." These little words allowed the sadistic racism of the South and the sophisticated racism of the North to circumvent the apparent good intention of the Warren court. Almost three decades have gone by and desegregation is still unrealized.

In 1955, Dr. Martin Luther King, Jr. led us into the era of the Civil Rights Movement. Hopes soared as the years went by, and we witnessed what appeared to be progress. The legal foundation of segregation was dismantled. In 1963, over 200,000 Black Americans and white Americans stood in the heat of an August sun and heard the Dreamer tell the world about his dream. As he articulated his dream in memorable cadence and rhythm and picturesque language, he seemed to speak for all Americans.

Hope soared even higher when the Civil Rights Voter Rights legislation was passed in 1964-65, the first in almost a hundred years, and added to all of that was the antipoverty program. We were on our way! At last America would "make real the promise of democracy." The huge man from Texas, who somewhere along the way had been converted from a sadistic racist to a shatterers of racism, had us dreaming of a Great Society. Everybody seemed to be dreaming wonderful dreams during those days. That is, almost everybody. Racism was not dead yet! Alas! Poor Lyndon Johnson, a giant of a man, was forced from office by a "nasty little war in Vietnam."

There was another voice in Washington in 1963 that warned that while King was having a dream, the masses of Black people were having nightmares. Malcolm X was in touch with the masses of Black people, particularly the young, and he knew that discontent was intensifying. We should have been wise enough to see that the political and social gains, as meager as they were, were way ahead of economic gains.

Frustration deepened, expectations were not being realized, so in 1966, in a sultry Alabama summer after a long hot march, Stokely Carmichael, then president of SNCC, hit a responsive chord with his cry, "Black Power." Incontrovertibly, the frustration was valid. In 1966, the President's commission reported:

> Hence, in 1966 despite eleven years of intense Civil Rights activity and the new anti-poverty programs, the median income of a Black family was only 58 percent of the income of an average White family, and Black unemployment still ran twice as high as White unemployment despite the war induced prosperity which the country was enjoying. In some categories, conditions were considerably worse. Unemployment among Black teenagers ran at 26 percent. In the Hough area of Cleveland, which experienced a rebellion in 1966 and again in 1968, Black unemployment in 1965 ran at 14 percent, only two percentage points below what it was in 1960. Another important indicator, the Black sub-employment rate, which reflects part time work, discouraged workers and low paid workers was 33 percent in 1966 in the "worst" areas of nine major cities.

The quality of education, despite some gains in the number of years of formal schooling attained remained low. Thus Black students tested out at substantially lower levels than white youths: up to three years difference in "level of achievement" among twelfth graders. Residential segregation proved to be the toughest nut for the integrationist movement to crack. In 1966, a special census taken in twelve cities revealed increased rates of segregation in eight of them.

A joint 1967 report by the U.S. Bureau of Labor Statistics and the Bureau of the Census, outlining the social and economic condition of Blacks in this country, concluded that "perhaps the most distressing evidence presented in this report indicates that conditions are stagnant or deteriorating in the poorest areas." In US cities the population of one million or more, the percentage of nonwhite families living in "poverty areas" between 1960 and 1966 remained constant at 34 percent. In New York and Chicago, however, the percentage increased. In Cleveland's Hough district, median family income declined over this same period. In the Watts district of Los Angeles, conditions also did not improve.

One of the sad and cruel developments of that time was what was called "white backlash." This was supposedly a warning to Blacks that they were arousing a generous, courageous, and powerful people to retaliate against what that people perceived to be the unreasonable demands and antagonistic militancy of Blacks. This further infuriated Black people. What unreasonable demands? Is seeking equal opportunity and justice after three hundred years of unrequited labor unreasonable? What militancy? If Black people were truly militant, insurrection and revolution would have been initiated a long time ago. Even Vice President Hubert Humphrey was saying in 1967, if he were treated as Black people are treated he would lead a rebellion himself. No! There was nothing new about the white backlash. It had always been there and probably would always be there. Only the name changed; the intent remains the same.

In 1968, Dr. Martin Luther King, Jr. was planning to return to Washington, this time to stay. For then he saw what was needed was a "radical redistribution of political and economic power." He never made it! A little while later, Bobby Kennedy was killed as he campaigned for the presidency, in Los Angeles. What a sobering time for America. President Kennedy, Malcolm X, Martin Luther King, Bobby Kennedy, noble spirits who probably had more in common than they realized, all of them trapped by the anticonstitutional, antihuman-rights forces that eventually killed them. The death of good men, the Vietnamese War, thousands of protestors in the streets,

Black rebellious reaction to the inability to see substantial change—
it was a time of upheaval. The nation turned to Nixon. It rejected
a good man, Hubert Humphrey, and elected a bad one.

1969—Black Solidarity Day

It does seem that in a time of crisis, where Black people are involved—especially when it seems we are getting something or we
are too militant—the nation turns to weak and questionable men.
But again, not only do Black people suffer as the nation turns back-
wards, white people suffer too. When will we learn that the absence of justice anywhere is the denial of justice everywhere.

The depth of Nixon's chicanery came to light in his second term.
There is a Biblical saying, "there is nothing hid that shall not be
brought to light." Watergate and all that it meant is forever recorded in American history. The revelation shocked Americans to
the core. The highest lawmakers and office holders in the land
were guilty of the most heinous crimes. It was to be revealed that
even the venerated FBI with its sainted leader, J. Edgar Hoover,
along with the CIA were guilty of the most horrible violations of
law and decency. It was a time when the rights of all Americans
were jeopardized. Spies, wire taps, snoopers were everywhere.
Dossiers and files were kept on everyone.

Nixon refused to give up the tapes, which were recorded some
of his devious deeds. "A constitutional crisis," America moaned.
Yes, responded Black people, but it did not begin with Nixon. It
began with slavery; it began with the "3/5 of a man" concept; and,
as far as Blacks are concerned, it has remained. In fact, as long as
it remains true for Blacks it will be true for all Americans. What
America must understand is that the periodic constitutional crises
which it experiences are a normal state of affairs for Black people.

The nation could not bring itself to vote for Gerald Ford. He
was a Nixon appointee. So it turned to Jimmy Carter. A decent
man, a believer in human rights with a heart as big as his grin. But,
he could not resolve the complexity of the hostage crisis, and the
myriad of other problems that troubled America. So they turned
him out after one term. One of the reasons believed by many
people, even by Carter himself, is that he was too cozy with Black
people. Andrew Young, a Black man, represented the U.S.A. at

the United Nations; Patricia Harris, a Black woman, was a cabinet member; Blacks seemed to be everywhere. Again, the progress was only illusion.

Consider what the president's own National Advisory Council on Economic Opportunity had to say in its final report (September 1981):

> We assert that there is another deep, unreported crisis going on in America today. It is the crisis in desperate lives of 55 million poor, and near poor citizens who go to bed each night not knowing whether they will have a job tomorrow, be able to pay the rent or doctor's bills, or feed the kids. There seems to be no "happy times" available for these people.

But time is getting short. And the burned out neighborhoods in Miami like Detroit, Watts, Cleveland from earlier years may well foreshadow the awful possibilities that lay before us if we continue to make the dignity of human life a secondary public concern. In this we recall the words of Dr. Martin Luther King, Jr. while organizing the Poor People's March when he stated "only a tragic death wish can prevent our nation from reordering its priorities."

Another report equally devastating is an article in the *New Jersey Record* (January 7, 1981), entitled "Black Children Face Tough Odds":

> Washington, D.C. —A black child in America has nearly one chance in two of being born in poverty and is twice as likely as a white baby to die during the first year of life. If the black child survives that first year, the odds are against him growing up healthy, wealthy, or wise.

Black children are more likely than white children to be sick and without regular sources of health care. They are three times as likely to be labeled mentally retarded, twice as likely to drop out of school before twelfth grade, and three times as likely to be unemployed.

A black teenager has a one-in-ten chance of getting into trouble with the law and is five times as likely as a white teenager to be murdered.

This bleak portrait based largely on government surveys drawn together in one report was presented yesterday by the Children's Defense Fund, a Washington-based lobbying and advocacy group for children.

The statistics "show why millions of black children lack self-confidence, feel discouragement, despair, numbness, or rage as they try to grow up on islands of poverty, ill health, inadequate education, squalid streets with dilapidated housing, crime, and rampant unemployment in a nation of boastful affluence," said the Fund's president, Marian Wright Edelman.

There is passing acknowledgment in the report that the last two decades have been years of progress for some blacks because of affirmative action programs, government scholarships, and court mandated desegregation; about one-third of black children who graduated from high school go on to college, about the same proportion as among white youth. But, Edelman contended, if the black middle class has grown, the black poor have increased at an even faster rate.

After a spurt of progress in the late sixties, gains made in lifting black children out of poverty leveled off. The seventies produced far more progress for the elderly than it did for black children, according to the statistics the Fund cited.

Clearly, the economic ravages of the last decade have had a particularly devastating impact on the black poor. Income for black households, adjusted for inflation, declined. In the sixties, the unemployment rate for black youth was twice as high as for white teenagers. Now, it is three times as high.

And the family structure of blacks appears to have been under even greater assault. Four of five white children live in two parent families, fewer than half of all black children do. Only one white child in 38 lives away from both parents; one in eight black children does. Proportionally, there are far more black children born to teenage mothers, far more black children in institutions.

Now building a full head of steam across the country, was the most conservative reactionary force seen in a long time. *Thunder on the Right* was the title of a book written by Alan Crawford exposing "The Politics of Resentment." The book identifies the Right's leaders and their procedures, organizations, lobbies, periodicals, think tanks, auxiliaries, and fund raisers. The book documents the computerization of this new movement's endeavors. Tied to the movement was God himself, at least according to a group that called itself the Moral Majority. The surge of this force was able to catapult Ronald Reagan into the presidency.

We should have anticipated that a movie star would become president. After all, America has always gone to Hollywood when reality became too troubling. It could have been John Wayne. But, he was dead and then when you add to the Hollywood syndrome the proclivity for the mean and narrow in time of crisis, we should have known it would be Ronald Reagan.

With Reagan's election, we immediately saw the similarity between him and Rutherford B. Hayes. Reagan and Rutherford kind of go together:

- a favoritism to the constitution resisters
- anti-busing; tax-exemption status to racist schools
- removal of legal protection
- decimation of voter rights

And the time that brought Reagan to power was so much like post-reconstruction. They call this movement the New Right, but there is really nothing new about it. During the early days of American history, it was manifest destiny. During the Civil War period, it was states rights or home rule. During the heyday of American capitalism, it was rugged individuals. During the sixties it was the white backlash. But, whatever it calls itself, it is and always has been anticonstitutional, anti-Black, anti-Latino, anti-Chicano, anti-Native Americans, anti-semitic, anti-Asian, anti-poor, antiwomen, anti-human rights.

They have always attracted to their ranks the KKK, the John Bircheres, the anti-semites. Everything crawls out of the holes and cemeteries when they make their move.

We must carefully observe the convergence of aforementioned the three categories of racism:

- *Sadistic*: significantly also including the rise of KKK activity.
- *Sophisticated*: big money, America's corporate giants pouring billions into this New Right movement.

- *Simple*: a great number of decent folks were carried along by the desire for change.

The surge of these three categories of racism defeated the shatterers of racism. We also need to observe a crisis of the electoral process: While Reagan's people were boasting of a mandate from the people, the truth of the matter, was that a significant number of Americans did not think it worth their while to participate. They simply did not vote.

There are two developments that make the New Right more menacing than ever before: economic crisis and conservative religion.

1. *Economic Crisis*

More serious than ever before, was and is the economic crisis. Ronald Reagan was supposed to balance the budget and lead us to new heights of prosperity. What we have experienced is a budget that gives meat to the rich and bones to the poor. "A jelly-bean budget," Vernon Jordan[4] called it. "A Jones Town budget,"[5] Lane Kirkland[6] called it. The problem with Kirkland's description is that at Jones Town the culprit drank the poison too. It isn't likely Reagan will take the medicine he is dishing out. Even the director of the Office of Management and the Budget, David Stockman, admitted that it was a rich-take-all budget wrapped up in new verbiage. What we have seen is a shift in the budget away from social programs to the military machine.

What is important to note that everybody is hurt by this budget except a very few, which again emphasizes the point continuously made: if the majority does not defend and promote the interest of the minority, eventually they will be in the same predicament. Corporations are closing and running off to other parts of the world in search of cheap labor. These are not good days for Americans, Blacks, or whites, Jews and non-Jews, religionists and non-religionist, young and old. In addition to the economic and social shock waves there are assaults on legal rights, not to mention human rights.

It cannot be overemphasized that an economic crisis brings out the worst in human beings. As the "Have a Little" experience a threat to their security, they turn on the "Have Nots" and/or Minorities, and fix the blame on them. If only the "Have a Little" would redirect their attention to the "Have a Plenty" and demand economic justice for all, including the "Have Nots," the crisis could be resolved.

But the "Have a Plenty" have such control over the media and other informing institutions that they can keep the "Have a Little" in ignorance concerning their best interest.

An impartial distant observer must ask why poor working people cannot see they share a common predicament and that if they entered into solidarity they could improve their lot a thousandfold, and if they coalesced with all other ordinary, decent, excluded, dispossessed, alienated people—blacks, whites, Chicano, Latino, Asian, Jews, students and intellectuals, men and women, young and old, all who share a desire for a better society, a more humane, truly democratic society—they could go a long way towards achieving their objective.

But, divided and suspicious of each other, manipulated by forces that profit from their fragmentation and distrust, they will always be weak and vulnerable to the shifts of powerful people, interests, and drives, and there will always be a constitutional crisis.

2. *Conservative Religion*

While fundamentalism and/or evangelism have always been politically ultra-conservative for most of America's history, they have exercised their influence subtly. Often times they have taken public stands against political involvement. But, even their silence has been acquiescence in the status quo, which has sustained their interest. So, in a real sense, there was no need to be politically involved.

Who can forget Billy Graham's friendship with Nixon, and Oral Roberts calling Nixon a praying man in September of the election year.

Significantly, Jerry Falwell, Billy Graham, Oral Roberts, and other electronic holy superstars have never taken a stand against racism, sexism, anti-semitism and never supported any causes or launched any movement against economic exploitation or political exclusion.

Where were they during the Civil Rights days? They were where they are and where conservative religionists have always been—on the side of the rich and the powerful. In foreign lands, they have stood with the colonizer and the most repressive dictatorial regimes. And in so doing, they have always been against poor people and minorities. They have made Christianity and capitalism synonymous. "Rugged individualism" translated in their jargon becomes "individual salvation"—purity of soul. They only want to purify the soul and deliver it safely to heaven. Never mind if the body is sick, ill-fed, homeless, poor, uneducated—especially if it is a Black or Brown or Red or Yellow body.

In recent times these non-political or apolitical religionists, who in times past silently and subtly supported the status quo, has come forth conspicuously to join the New Right—bringing all their resources when them. In American history, where super-patriotism joins hands with super-religion Black and poor are in super-trouble. Remember when Nixon and his men use to wear the little American flag in their lapels? They were super-patriotic. Remember when the missionaries went to Africa to bring the blessing of Christianity to the Dark Continent? "When they came, we had the land and they had the Bible," said the despondent African, "Now we have the Bible and they have the land."

Remember the Southern sheriff who boasted he liked nothing better than "Bible reading, prayer meetings, Sunday service, and beating niggers"? Remember Southern America and South Africa boast the greatest proliferation of Christianity?

This situation prevails because, in spite of the Evangelical profession of Biblical faith and trust in Jesus Christ, they have interpreted both according to their culture and interest.

The God of the Bible is the God who identifies with the poor and dispossessed, who takes side with the oppressed against the oppressor, who is angry with the wicked everyday—and the wicked here is not some poor soul guilty of stealing a pocket book and knocking somebody in the head (probably a member of his own race). The wicked here are the exploiters who steal lands and countries, oil wells and diamond mines. The wicked here is the colonizer who takes the wealth of countries to enhance his mother country. The wicked here are those who create political, economic, social systems which deny justice, opportunity, and human rights. Yes! The God of the Bible calls powerful individuals and oppressive institutions into judgement.

He even says to the pious religionists, Stop your singing, praying, and fasting, cease your religious exercises until justice rolls down like water, righteousness like a mighty stream; Clothe the naked, feed the hungry, and take care of the widows.

WHAT SHALL WE DO?

It must be clear from what we have seen that we face terrifying adversary, an adversary that has never given up on its desire to make over the world in general, and the U.S.A. in particular, in its own image, an image of reaction—racism; an image which, if implemented, will mean political, economic, and social impoverishment for all but a few of their own kind.

How shall we do battle with this powerful adversary? A few moments ago, I asked "To whom shall we trust our constitutional or human rights? Since presidents and courts, and congresses have all been at one time or another anti-black and therefore anti-constitutional."

The answer is we must trust the people and we must trust the Creator. I will not attempt to apply a name or even a gender to the Creator. Suffice it to say, for the moment, we must have faith in a good, principled universe which is purposeful. We must find the keys to build the mightiest coalition. There were two notable times in American History when it almost happened. The Populist Movement in the first quarter of the nineteenth century, when poor whites and poor blacks formed the basis of solidarity derived from their mutual exploitation; then again, during the Civil Rights, era when labor, liberal whites, students, scholars, and religionists joined with Blacks and made some social and political progress before the movement was beaten back.

Now, today, we must identify the factors and forces, the individuals and institutions and organizations, and build a coalition that will generate and direct the mightiest movement the nation has ever seen, and not just to defeat the New Right, but to shape a better society. A society where justice and equality are extended to all. Where the constitution is defended, promulgated, and practiced. A society in which all people participate equally in and benefit equally from the economic, political, and social structure.

Indeed, a society of the people, by the people, and for the people.

With faith in the people and faith in the Almighty, *we can do it, and we will do it!*

Notes

1. John Hope Franklin, *From Slavery to Freedom* (New York: Alfred A. Knopf, 1980), p. 243.
2. *Ibid.*, p. 255.
3. *Ibid.*, p. 254.
4. Vernon Jordan was the president of the Urban League from 1972 to 1981.
5. Jonestown was the site of the mass suicide that took place in Guiana in 1978 by the cult followers of evangelist Jim Jones.
6. Lane Kirkland was the presidents of AFL-CIO from 1979 to 1995.

PART II

HISTORY OF RACISM OR COLOR PREJUDICE

J. A. Rogers, the eminent, pioneering, but little known African-American historian, probably did the most exhaustive writing on racism. In his book, *Nature Knows No Color Line,* he identifies five instances of color prejudice among different peoples, starting from the earliest in India.

India

The first or the earliest instance was in India over 5,000 years ago, when the Aryas or Aryans invaded the Indus Valley and found there a black people, the Dasysus or Dasyus.

The Aryan conquerors did what was to be repeated throughout history. After they defeated the Dasysus (or Dravidians, as they became known), the Aryans stole, distorted, and destroyed their history, then promoted the lie that the vanquished were barbarians, or savages, or at the least bereft of achievement.

Yet the Dravidians had a significant civilization, as evidenced in the fact that the Buddha came from them. Godfrey Higgins, as quoted by Rogers, writes:

> The religion of Buddha of India is well-known to have been very ancient. In the most ancient temples scattered throughout Asia where his worship still continues he is found as yet with the flat face, thick lips and curly hair of the Negro. Several statues of his may be met in the Museum of the East India Company. The religion of the Negro God is found in the ruins of his temple and other circumstances to have

> been spread over an immense extent of country, even to the remotest parts of Britain and to have been professed by devotees, inconceivably numerous. That the Buddhists were Negroes the icons of their God clearly prove.[1]

The offspring of the Aryans have been stealing, distorting, and destroying Black people's history since time immemorial, as I shall document as I proceed. In addition, color prejudice is found in Aryan writings. In the *Rigveda* (Book 14, Hymn 42:1), Indra, their national god, is depicted as "blowing away with supernatural might from earth and from heavens the Black skin which Indra hates." India's caste system was based on color. The word *varna* (caste) literally means "color." *Arya varna* (white skin) and *Krishna varna* (black skin).

Rabindranath Tagore, Indian poet and Nobel Prize laureate, as quoted by J.A. Rogers, writes:

> Our own history began with it and though India desperately tried some kind of mechanical race adjustment she has failed in giving birth to a living political organism owning to this abnormal caste consciousness that obstructs the strain of human sympathy and spirit of mutual cooperation.[2]

Egypt

The second instance of color prejudice was in ancient Egypt. Depending on who was in power, there was either the "evil race of Kush," referring to Black people, or the pale, degraded race of *Aryad*, referring to whites. It is generally agreed that color even came to reach the level found in India. Whites did not arrive in Egypt in any great numbers until the Ptolemaic invasion of the third century B.C.

Jews

J.A. Rogers wrote that "The third instance of color prejudice is to be found in the rabbinical writings. The early rabbis did very definitely and abundantly say that a black skin was the result of a "curse" on Ham by Noah. The signs of this "curse," according to certain rabbis, were "a black skin, misshapen lips, and twisted hair."

The Bible says the "curse" was placed on Canaan, Ham's son,

but some rabbis said it was placed directly on Ham. Rabbi Huja maintains that Ham came forth from the Ark "black skinned." This would mean that Ham, who had gone into the Ark fair-skinned, had undergone this change of color in only the one hundred and ninety days that they had been in the Ark. Ham, it appears, had been guilty of some sexual infraction while in the Ark.

Topinard, a French anthropologist, thinks, too, that the rabbis of the first century were the first to stress differences of race and color. Race, as we now use it, he says, was unknown in far antiquity, at least in the West. He correctly notes that Aristotle and Hippocrates do not mention race, though both studied anatomy and the then-known varieties of the human race, including the Negro.

The Greeks had two distinct divisions of humanity—Greek and barbarian, that is, citizen and alien. An Athenian who married an alien, regardless of color, was sold into slavery. It was for a long time the same in Rome. "Race," as based on color and physique, is, in fact, comparatively recent. The King James Bible of the seventeenth century does not mention it. Shakespeare used it only for family lineage contexts. So also does the first English dictionary by Nathaniel Bailey in 1736, and the second by Dr. Samuel Johnson in 1750.[3]

To quote Topinard,

> In the first century when Christianity was beginning to seat itself in Rome the doctrine of a separate creation for whites and blacks was defended by the Babylonian rabbis and later by Emperor Julian. In 415 A.D., when one council was debating whether the Ethiopians were descended from Adam and the theory they weren't was making progress, St. Augustine in his 'City of God' intervened and declared that no true Christian would doubt that all men, of no matter what form, color, or height were of the same protoplasmic origin.[4]

Why, we are forced to ask, did the rabbis put the curse on black-skinned Ham. It is clear from the scripture that the curse was on Canaan (Genesis 9:24, 25). Also, it has been pointed out that, next to the Aryans, the Jews were more color-conscious than any of the ancients. What were the reasons?

According to the Bible, the Jews were called Hebrews, meaning, among other things, one who crosses over (referring to the fact that they crossed over the Euphrates River) and/or Israelites (a prince of God or one who has power with God, a name given to Jacob, the second son of Israel after he had wrestled, or prayed with God all night long [His name was changed from deceiver to Israel.]) It wasn't until the Babylonian captivity in 605, that they were called Jews, according to the Bible. These people, Jews or Hebrew Israelites, had spent four hundred years in Egypt, and it is generally conceded that Egypt was a Black country.

There were seventy Isrealites going into Egypt, fleeing a famine. When they departed there were hundreds of thousands. Obviously the Israelites had assimilated the culture of Egypt, and there was widespread miscegenation. So, it can be logically concluded that the seventy who went into Egypt, whatever their nationality and color, would be Black Egyptians (or Africans) when they departed. In addition, the great accomplishments of the Egyptians would be stolen, adopted, or assimilated.

We must remember that hundreds of years before the Israelite nomads came out of the desert, Africans had already developed religious systems, including monotheism. They were practicing circumcision and offering sacrifices to gods. They knew mathematics, engineering, and architecture, as evidenced in the great pyramids and other huge structures. So extraordinary are these structures that some writers wrote that they were done by visitors from outer space. They knew biology and medicine long before Hippocrates. They knew agriculture, navigation, and astronomy.

Africans have never been given credit for these accomplishments. The point is, why would these people who were obviously dark-skinned pronounce a curse on dark skin. In fact, many believed—at that time and during this time—that the Jews were African.

There is a belief that the Jews were African. The answer rests among these considerations, discussed by J.A. Rogers:

1. They had been enslaved by black Egyptians and Ethiopians.
2. After they were settled in Canaan (Palestine) they were twice invaded by Egyptians and Ethiopians. Shishak, Ethiopian ruler of Egypt, ravaged the land, plundered Solomon's temple, and

took a great number of Jews as slaves to Egypt (II Chronicles 12). Another Ethiopian King, Zera, who came with "a host of a thousand and three hundred chariots," was beaten off (II Chronicles 14).

3. It could be that before the Jews left Egypt they could have assimilated some of the color prejudice already mentioned.

4. Another consideration is that once the Israelites were far removed from their Egyptian experience and began to mingle with fair-skinned people, they sought to explain the origin of Black people, so they invented the story.

5. Black skin could now be singled out for retribution, a slave of slaves, because of what Egyptians and Ethiopians had done to them.

6. Probably the strongest reason is that the Israelites wanted Canaan's land, believing that they had the blessing of Jehovah, their God, to take the land because Canaan and all Blacks were cursed.

Did Europeans not do the same with Indians and Africans? Their God had ordained that they conquer them and take their land. So Africans and Indians were cursed savages.

The Arabs, who are related to the Jews, had their problem with color also. In their version of the Ham story, it applied to the Blacks of the Sudan. There is the story that Mahomet once stopped at a woman's house and asked her how many sons she had. She had three, but, fearing that Mahomet would take one to carry his baggage, she hid one and brought out two.

The prophet of God, knowing that she had lied, placed a curse upon the hidden son. While two sons would be fair-skinned children who would be wealthy and rulers of the earth, the hidden son would be as black as darkness, and his children would be sold like cattle and become perpetual slaves to their brothers.[5]

Let me state emphatically that these myths/legends did not represent the thinking and attitude of the overwhelming majority of the devotees of those religions. A Christian slave on becoming Muslim was free, and he and his descendants were eligible for the highest office in the state. On the other hand, Christianity made no difference in the status of an African slave in America. Truth demands that I confess that the Christian slave among the so-called barbarians of Africa were treated with more humanity than the African slaves among the Christians in the so-called civilized world.

Before I move on to color prejudice in Rome and America, I should point out that blacks had their color prejudice also. Incidentally, the blacks had their own theory of the origin of the whites. Thin lips, straight hair, and a white skin, they said, originated from an albino ape, who was the ancestor of the whites. Christianized Negroes, dipping into the Bible, had their origin of the whites, too. All men, they said, were originally black, but, when God shouted at Cain in the Garden of Eden for having killed Abel, he turned white from fright. The rabbis, on the other hand, said that Cain turned black, as a curse.

Certain American Negroes also believe that a white skin was caused from leprosy. The ancestor of the whites, they say, was Gehazi, servant of Elisha, who was cursed with leprosy for having solicited money from Naaman (II Kings 5:21).

Some Negro preachers and expounders of the Bible have even proved that white people will not go to heaven because Jesus placed a curse on their hair. As authority they quote the parable of the sheep and the goats (Matthew 25:32), where Christ said that when he comes again in all his glory he shall separate the sheep from the goats, place the sheep on his right hand and say to them, "Come ye blessed of my Father, inherit. Come in the kingdom prepared for you from the foundation of the world." Now there is this distinction: The goats have straight hair like the whites; the sheep, woolly, like the blacks. [6]

Xenophane of 550 B.C. rightly observed that men made their gods in their own image, and that the gods of the Ethiopians were black and flat nosed like themselves. Marco Polo said that the "natives of Malabar make their devils white and their saints black" like themselves.

Mungo Park said that the Africans accounted for his white skin by saying that as a baby he had been continually dipped in milk. The prominence of his nose, they said, was due to its being pinched daily "until it acquired its present unnatural and unsightly shape." Parkyn, a white traveler, said that Ethiopians said he had "cat's" eyes and "monkey hair" and that he had "lost his skin." [7]

Another belief was (and still is) that a white skin was the result of leprosy. The French philosopher Voltaire thought that African albinos were descended from "a race that had been whitened by leprosy." Many East Indians still believe that white people are the descendants of lepers. T.S. Ramanujam says, "An Indian villager after seeing an Englishman for the first time asked me whether the gentleman was tainted with leprosy." Harold Cox tells of a high-caste Indian woman who, on seeing white persons for the first time, said, "Why they have no skins."[8]

Rome

The fourth stage of color prejudice occurred in Rome. J.A. Rogers writes:

> The fourth stage in the development of color prejudice seemed therefore to have occurred in Rome of the first century A.D. as a phase of the fight between Christianity and Paganism. Prior to that, however, [the] Pagan master held the belief that humanity, regardless of color, were Roman or Barbarian. Christianity, the new religion, decided that of one blood God made all the peoples of the earth and that all men were brothers in Christ. Moreover, the earliest Christians pictured the Virgin Mary and Christ as black, both being an evolution of the worship of Isis and Horus, which was once common in Rome.[9]

Concerning prejudice among the Spaniards, Portugese, Anglo-Saxons, French, and Dutch in the Americas, Rogers wrote:

> Color prejudice was never so strong among Spaniards and Portugese in the Americas as among the Anglo-Saxons. They had not only been living among black people from the earliest times (as will be seen later) but were considered mixed with them. The Spaniards treated the dark skinned Indians of the West Indies very cruelly but this was not so much white imperialism as it was Christian imperialism. The Indians were "ungodly heathen" and the Spaniards felt that God had delivered them into their hands, precisely as did the dark-skinned Jews when they entered Canaan, firmly believing that their Jehovah had delivered the Amalekites, Jebusites, and others in their hands to be slaughtered.
>
> For cruelty based on color, the French in Haiti came first,

the Dutch in Guyana, second, and the English in the West Indies, third. The last, greater sticklers for law and morality, found greatest justification for their treatment of the blacks in the "curse" on Ham.[10]

Science of Physiognomy

Why was color prejudice so difficult in the Americas? Consider these answers. White prejudice against Blacks may be rooted in or influenced by the study in physiognomy, which judges character according to physical traits. According to Rogers:

> It is quite possible also that the color prejudice of white for black began in prejudice among the whites for shades of their own color. I refer to the so-called science of Physiognomy, which rates individuals as good or bad, desirable or undesirable, on their physical traits. This pseudo science probably originated in the East.
>
> A very ancient Indian work, Elem-I-Kaifa, tells how to judge character by the eyes, height, hair, color, and so on. But the work to which it owes development and power in the West was Aristotle's Physiognomica of the fourth century B.C. , Soft, silky hair, said Aristotle, was a sign of cowardice. Coarse ones meant courage, except when it curled too much, or was "wooly like that of the Ethiopians"; then it signified the same as the soft, silky one. A full voice, deep and round, indicated courage; a languid or high-pitched one, cowardice. Short arms showed addiction to gambling and dancing. A pale complexion, small eyes, and thick black hair on the body showed lasciviousness. Big feet meant strength of character, provided the toes did not curve at the ends in which case it indicated impudence. Bony buttocks showed strong character; fat ones, a weak mind. A large head was quickness; a small forehead, stupidity; grey eyes, cowardice. As for the nose, its shape, size, width, had great effect on one's character.
>
> Blondeness so much valued in the United States was no more desirable to the Greeks than jet black, according to Aristotle. He said, "Too black a hue marks the coward as witness Egyptians and Ethiopians; so also, does too white a complexion as you may see from women. So the hue that makes for courage must be intermediate between these ex-

tremes. A tawny color indicates a bold spirit as in lions but too ruddy a hue makes a rogue." That is, the Greeks seem to have thought that the most desirable color was a dark brunette, or mulatto one. By "too white a color" he undoubtedly meant the fair whites of the north. In his politics he classed them as inferior.

The Greeks admired physical strength and muscles do show up better in a dark skin than a fair one. Julian Huxley, a great living scientist, says, "Why does a good physique look better when the skin over the muscles is black than when it is white? And we say, today, not tall, blonde and handsome, but tall, dark and handsome."[11]

Physiognomy grew so strong in Europe that in 1559 Pope Paul IX was forced to write about it. In 1743, the British Parliament outlawed it. While these efforts lessened the impact in Europe, in America it continued to grow. Since Christianity was professed to be the religion of most colonists, the Bible was used to buttress Black inferiority. The curse on Ham was played with great vigor. Thereby, there was the revival of the doctrine or theory of dual creation.

In 1655, Isaac de la Peyrere wrote a book entitled *The Pre-Adamite*. He argued that there were two creations in the Book of Genesis. Chapters One and Two speak of the creation of man, and later, after the making of man from the dust of the earth, this man was given a companion. Adam and Eve were their names. The other creation was therefore pre-Adamic—it was from this creation that obtained his wife. Adam and Eve were created exclusively to be ancestors of God's chosen people, the Jews.

Pope Alexander VIII thought this rank heresy and had de la Peyrere thrown into the dungeon at Versailles. The book was burned and, prostrating himself before the Pope and renouncing the doctrine, the author escaped the fate that befell others who promulgated things the Roman Catholic Church did not like.

Africans had been in the Americas or so-called New World centuries before Columbus and Columbus' ancestors, as documented in Dr. Ivan Van Sertima's great book, *They Came Before Columbus*. Rogers quotes Harvard professor Leo Wiener, who wrote:

> The presence of Negroes before Columbus is proved by the representation of Negroes in American sculpture and design; by the occurence of a black nation at Darien early in the 16th Century and more specifically by Columbus' emphatic reference to Negro traders from Guinea (Ghana), who trafficked in gold alloy of precisely the same composition and bearing the same name (Guanin), is frequently referred to by early writers on Africa.[12]

Columbus in his third voyage tells of seeing blacks, and Balboa, in 1513, said he saw Africans in Panama. Moreover, Africans were with the early explorers and adventurers including Columbus. Richio Alzo Ninu was navigator on the flagship on which Columbus sailed to the New World. In fact, it is probable that Columbus learned about the New World and how to get there from Africa. For eight hundred years the Moors had ruled Spain, and Columbus was in West Africa just before he sailed for America.

Also, Africans were with Balboa when he reached the Pacific Ocean, with Ponce de Leon when he reached Florida Easter Sunday 1512, and with Hernado De Soto when he reached America. They were with d'Ayllon in 1526 when he landed at St. Elena in the Carolinas and started a colony at San Miguel, the same place where the English founded Jonestown 83 years later. They were with De Narvaez in 1527 when a ship wreck killed all but four. Among the survivors was Estevanico, a Black, who then traveled from Florida to California, crossing the Mississippi 150 years before La Salle. Estevanico then led expeditions from Mexico City that discovered Arizona and New Mexico in 1540. Africans were among early settlers, as in the case of San Miguel.

Africans had been accepted in the Old World: As already mentioned, the Moors ruled Spain for eight hundred years, lifting it from the pit of barbarism to the pinnacle of high culture. In England, France, Germany, Russia, indeed, all over Europe, Africans were accepted and, in fact, attained high status in these countries, as documented in J.A. Rogers's three volume work *Sex and Race*, and in Dr. Ivan Sertima's *The African in Early Europe*.

During ancient times, Africans were highly regarded. The two leading nations "white western civilization" prized so highly—Rome and Greece—were deeply involved with Africans. After all, Hannibal with his Black troops had crossed the Alps and marched on Rome, then remained in Italy for many years. The largest physical part of the Roman Empire was in Africa, and there were three African popes—Victor I, Miltiades, and Galasisu I. The Greeks viewed the Egyptians with such esteem that many of their scholars studied in Egypt — and stole from their works. George James, in his book *Stolen Legacy,* documented Africa as the source of Greeks philosophical and mathematical systems.

And finally, wonder of wonders, Africans held slaves right here in America. Virginia passed laws five times prohibiting the purchase of white people by Negroes.[13]

So the color stigma was not always the rule in America. So what happened? Whence came color prejudice? Whence came racism? Let us hold answers, and explore the prior questions: Who came to America and why?

A Gentlemen adventurers came. They were relatively few; they came for loot and didn't intend to stay long.

B. Fewer still come for adventure. They didn't stay long either.

C. Some came as settlers. There are five categories in this group:

1. There were the seekers after freedom.
   They came voluntarily, hoping to establish a better life. They were relatively few in number; let me emphasize, the true honest freedom-seekers who came to America were, relatively speaking, few in numbers.

2. There were indentured servants.
   Indentured servants were those who worked for a specified time to earn enough money to make a better life for themselves. They were not in great numbers. They came of their own free will; however, there were some who were forced.

3. There were the kidnapped.
   Male and female, Black and white, adults and children were stolen from different parts of the world. They came against their will. They, too, were relatively few in numbers.

4. There were the convicts, demented, prostitutes, and outcasts. They came in great numbers. The outcasts of Europe were expected to people the New World. They were
given a choice: continuing incarceration, for some even
facing the gallows or the guillotine, or going to the New
World. They chose the New World. They came in droves.

In 1611, Governor Dole urged James I to transport all
condemned persons to Virginia before that they were
shipped to India. The committee of Trade of New York
petitioned the authorities to send to New York all prisoners
to be transported from Newgate Prison. Nobody else from
the white laboring class was prepared to open up West
Virginia. The *American Historical Review* states that the
transportation of convicts was a regular and systematic
procedure through the seventeenth and eighteenth centuries. An estimated 20,000 of these convicts came to Maryland alone between 1737 and 1767.[14]

Also, the New World provided England an opportunity
to get rid of their loose women. The first ones who came
were probably of this class.

Narcissus Luttrell, writing in his diary, Thursday, 17 No-
vember 1692, tells of eighty such women being sold to Virginia. He mentions a ship going to Virginia in which the
magistrates had ordered 50 lewd women out of the House
of Correction and thirty others who walked the streets after ten o'clock at night. He mentioned another shipment of
Scottish prostitutes in 1695.[15]

The colonists complained bitterly that the criminal element was causing havoc in the country. It was not right
for Europe to empty its refuse on America (Gift 32).

Dr. Samuel Johnson said in 1769, "They [the Ameri-
cans] are a race of convicts and ought to be thankful for
anything we allow them short of hanging."[16] It should be
stated here that even the early pilgrims were no paragons
of virtue. Governor Bradford of New England, writing in
1642, said:

> And yet all this [severity of punishment] could not
> suppress the breaking out of sundry notorious sin,

especially drunkenness and uncleanliness, not only
incontinence between persons unmarried, for which
many both men and women have been punished
sharply, but some married persons, but that which is
even worse, sodomy . . . .[17]

England continued to empty her jails into America until
1783. Once America had declared her independence, ad-
ditional shiploads of convicts were refused entry. As a result, London's Newgate Prison overflowed.
In our time we have seen similar situations when Fidel
Castro allowed Cubans to come to America. Some said
he opened the jail cells and hospital rooms to send the worst
elements. Eventually, he was asked to take them back.
Imagine year after year of this kind of influx upon a society.

5.   And finally, the Africans came. Some came to make a
      better life. It has been argued that chattel slavery did not
      exist until 1659 or 1682. By then, Africans were scattered
      about the New World, building and exploring. But most
      came as slaves. In great numbers they came. What a
      mind-blowing consideration, the early population of the New
      World was primarily made up of criminals and Africans.
      Now why was that?

Let us remember that the New World was not a paradise. There
were endless miles of wilderness. Trees had to be cut and made
into lumber. Roads had to be carved out, and planting, harvesting,
and building had to be done. So much work, not just hard work, but
complicated work. It required laborers who were strong, and also
knowledgeable and experienced in various techniques and skills.
Not only were skill and ability required but also stamina and forti-
tude. Then there was always the danger of attacks from betrayed
and butchered Native Americans. Who would want to come to
such a place? Surely not those who were stable and satisfied in
their homeland. And it would be that element which would have
the skill and know-how necessary for survival. So that left, for the
most part, the unsavory element.

Another reason Europe would not send its able-bodied, decent citizens was because of the wars. The Thirty Year War (1618-1648) had taken its toll on England and France. The War of the Spanish Succession also helped to deplete the population. So that left the unsavory element, for the most part, to people the New World. But there was one land that had an abundance of human kind.

The African was ideal for the situation. They came from a continent with a long history of agriculture, mining, engineering, navigating, hunting, fishing, weaving, carving; they also came from intricate governments and family structures, a long history of socialization of respect and appreciation. They were perfect for skills and socialization. Who else could do the work necessary and bear the hardship and the dangers? The gentlemen settlers could not do it. It was so difficult that in Virginia 44 of the pilgrim fathers died in their first winter in America, and only 50 remained. Of that number only six or seven sound persons.

Convicts and misfits were surely not up to the task. They were cutthroats, murderers, thieves; what did they know about planting and building? And their weak frames could not take the hardship and work even if they had the mind and skill to, which they did not. That left the Native Americans, and they were unable and or unwilling to do the work. The Spaniards considered the Indians a step above the beast, so they tortured and murdered them. It was Bishop Las Casa (1474 - 1566) who could no longer stomach the cruelty to Indians, so he suggested African slaves be used; thus he could save the Indians. He later regretted his suggestion.[18] So the African became the ideal person for the special needs of the New World.

It is far within the mark to say that in time the African became the American economy. The survival and progress of the colonial experiment rested in their heads and on their backs and in their hands.

The labor of the Africans now became the most important single factor in the development of the New World. On them fell the crude work. And more than a little of the skilled ones. Some had brought with them their ancient skills in metal, weaving, carving, and agriculture. And as a colony grew, so grew the call for them. Nations fought one another on the high seas to seize their cargo of

Africans. The Dutch counted heavily on such captures for their colony of New Netherland.[19]

Rogers cites an experiment in the Georgia colony. The attempt was made to colonize without Africans. The experiment came to a crashing failure. Finally, they had to bring in the Africans. The colony boomed, and Georgia was able to make its contribution to the Revolutionary War. What made the African so important is that he was both capital and labor. A healthy, intelligent slave could bring as much as two thousand dollars. In 1785, Virginia valued her slaves at 6,370,400 pounds sterling or $31,292. According to Thomas Jefferson there were 270,762 of them. The free population, of whom some were African, was 292,852.[20]

The framers of the Constitution agreed the slave was 3/5 of a man. Slave trade not only made the African essential because of labor and capital within the colonies, but also Africans became the centerpiece in trade, from which springs so many industries. When the demand for slaves become so great, the British Parliament passed a law opening the trade to all her citizens. New England jumped in with both feet and eventually become dominant in the New World and in time rivaled the mother country. New England discovered that molasses, a key ingredient in rum-making, was being thrown away in the French Caribbean and, therefore, could be purchased cheaply. So with the French molasses, they were able to make rum and thus began what came to be called the Triangle Trade. Molasses produced in the Caribbean would be shipped to New England, where rum was made, then sent to Africa, where the rum with the other commodities would be traded for slaves who, in turn, were carried to the Caribbean to pick up the molasses, which was brought to New England, and begin the cycle again.

Astronomical wealth accrued to New England in particular and to the New World in general from the slave trade. In fact, Western civilization profited immensely from the slave trade. Eric Williams's book *Slavery and Capitalism* documents the slave trade as the foundation of European economy, and in fact everything else rested upon Africa. See also Walter Rodney's book *How Europe Underdeveloped Africa* for a wealth of information on this subject.

Karl Marx said, "the population and wealth of England after slumbering for seven hundred years began to develop itself under the influence of slave-acquired capital."[21]

Reparations

Now given the immense wealth made from the African, both from his person and his labor, one would have thought that when liberation came there would have been a special financial consideration accorded them, at the least, humane treatment. Neither occurred: Africans were never paid reparations nor treated humanely even to the present.

During Reconstruction (1865-1875) there was an effort made by a few. The Freedman's Bureau was created to assist the recently emancipated slaves. The 13th, 14th, and 15th Amendments to the Constitution were passed. The nation opened the door for political participation, and it seemed at last democracy and decency had arrived. Blacks responded with great enthusiasm and made great contributions. Free public schools in the South was one of the contributions. There were two Black U.S. senators: Blanche K. Bruce and Hiram R. Revels. There were Black congressmen and Black participation at all levels of government, but the slave masters were not finished. Rutherford B. Hayes, as a presidential candidate, had agreed to a compromise by which he would get the Southern whites' votes. Once he was elected, he would pull out troops and federal Marshalls from the South, this effectively handing over the South to the former slave masters.

By 1889 all the gains of Reconstruction were wiped out. The *Plessy v. Ferguson* decision, making "separate but equal" the law of the land, signaled another turn toward denial for Blacks. In 1890, Bishop McNeil Turner was arguing for reparations. His demand was $100 million, a modest sum indeed. Given the state of the country at that time, the proverbial snowball in hell had a better chance than reparations for Blacks.

In fact, Blacks could not get humane treatment, let alone reparations. There are those who are still arguing for reparations, and there is historical precedence: the Jews in Germany and, more recently, the Japanese in America. I think most of us would settle for a good affirmative action program. If the set-aside were honored, we would settle for that. Now the Supreme Court in its recent decision has made that exceedingly difficult to achieve. Set-asides and fair, decent treatment still eludes us.

New England

The success of New England in the slave trade produced envy and resentment among the slave-trading big wigs in Bristol, Liverpool, as well as the British Government and the British West Indies. The New Englanders were buying their molasses from the French Caribbean, and this was especially resented by the British Government, after all, France was an arch rival, and the British West Indies felt betrayed that their molasses was not being purchased by their own countrymen. There were unsuccessful attempts to resolve the matter in 1733, when the Parliament passed the molasses act. The New Englanders cried that this law would bankrupt them, so they disobeyed, and tension mounted.

In 1764, the Peace of Paris had just ended Britain's long war with France and Spain and left England in dire need of revenue to pay her huge national debt. America, meanwhile, was growing more and more prosperous. The British press and Parliament demanded that America be made to help with the debt. Interest in the Molasses—or Sugar—Act was revived. Britain sent out 27 warships to patrol the New England coast and soldiers and revenue agents to enforce the Act. The Americans at once felt the effects. Tempers waxed hot, and there was talk of war and independence. So here the seeds for the Revolutionary War were sown. It was really not the Tea Act but the Sugar Act that brought the war.[22]

What a fascinating consideration: the African and Africa were not only the source of wealth, the very life-line of Europe and America, but here, now, we see that if there had been no Africa, it is conceivable there would have been no America. And to further heighten the irony, the first to fall in America's opposition to Britain, which escalated into revolution, was a black man, Crispus Attucks, on March 5, 1770. What a debt Europe and America owe Africa and African people!

Now let us return to the question, Why color prejudice or racism in Euro-American history? The answer is: the need for justification. Somehow good Christians, as most whites considered themselves, had to find a way to square with their Christianity the brutal reality of slavery. So they reasoned that Africans were not human as they were, but subhuman, savages, heathens who really benefitted from their Christian benevolence. In some instances they saw it as a necessity that produced a substantial good, and therefore could be endured. In the Georgia experiment to which I have already referred, Reverend George Whitfield was opposed to slavery. He was a Wesleyan, and John Wesley hated slavery. It should be stated here that not all Europeans condoned or participated in slavery; many hated it and fought against it.

But when it seemed that the Georgia experiment would fail, Reverend Whitfield reluctantly went along with the use of slaves, saying:

> Hot countries can be cultivated with Negroes. What a flourishing country Georgia might have been had the use of them been permitted years ago! How many white people have been destroyed for want of them and how many thousands of pounds spent to no purpose at all.[23]

Then, there was that immoral element, consisting of those who had become used to the life of ease and wealth built on the backs and minds of Africans. They were not about to let it slip through their fingers for bad or evil. They had never had it so good, and being without morality and decency, they stamped the African a savage, brought to earth for their own special needs. Most went along with this doctrine concerning the treatment of Africans. How strange! Here were Europeans fresh from jail cells and lunatic houses — thieves, cut-throats, and murderers — dirty, diseased, and demented, enslaving blacks who were brought from countries without bars or bolts, and calling them savages.

I used to wonder how could a people be so mean and cruel to another people who had diligently worked the land and loyally defended it with their blood? But when I studied who it was that came to America, it became understandable. These were the villains, killers without feeling, compassion, or fairness for anybody. And since they were the majority, they had things pretty much their own way; the few (relatively speaking) decent folks were not about to challenge the system; in fact, they enjoyed and benefitted from the whole thing, not only they but their offspring too, up to the present time. Incontrovertibly European white-Christian civilization is still reaping the benefit of African enslavement.

So color prejudice became embedded in what was an economic venture, and racism was born. Those who came later inherited the lies, distortion, and culture. Until today African people in most quarters are viewed as immoral parasites. The magnificent history of Africa is not known, and the contribution of African people to America, indeed, to white civilization in general, is hidden from the light. It is true there is much that ails African people, but given what African people have been through, the wonder is not that we come up short in many areas; the wonder is that we survived at all. And even more than that, the wonder of wonders is that we are still making progress. Before the European, Africa had no history of criminal behavior, not of the kind we see in America today. Nor did the Native American. While we do not want to excuse personal irresponsibility, there is something wrong with the system.

Until we recognize that, we will never find the solution. Two things are necessary to end racism:

1. Tell the truth about history; rewrite the history books so that truth can get a hearing. This would tremendously impact on the people. It will humble some and exonerate others, but the truth is the light, and in the long run all will be the better for it.

2. Let's have a Marshall Plan, a real war on poverty. Let the nation invest the necessary resources, human and otherwise, to correct this age-old problem, and promote a better day, for all African people surely deserve it. If, however, morality or altruism cannot motivate, then be moved by enlightened self-interest. No nation can survive with such appalling poverty stripping the masses and such opulence for the upper classes. In the words of the activists, "No justice, no peace!"

Notes

1. J.A. Rogers, *Nature Knows No Color Line*, 3rd ed. (New York: Helga M. Rogers, 1952), p. 8.
2. Ibid.
3. Ibid., pp. 9, 10.
4. Ibid., p. 10.

5. Ibid., p. 13.
6. Ibid, p. 14.
7. Ibid., p. 14.
8. Ibid., p. 13, 14.
9. Ibid., P. 11.
10. Ibid., pp. 21, 22.
11. Ibid., p. 17.
12. J.A. Rogers, *Africa's Gift to America* (New York: Helga M. Rogers, 1961), p. 17
13. Ibid., p. 61.
14. Ibid., p. 31.
15. Ibid., p. 32.
16. Ibid.
17. Ibid., p. 33.
18. Ibid., 36.
19. Ibid.
20. Ibid., pp. 37, 38.
21. Ibid., p. 40.
22. Ibid., p. 42.
23. Ibid., p. 38.

CHAPTER THREE

PART I
STRENGTHENING THE BLACK COMMUNITY

PART II
FROM VICTIMS TO VICTORS

STRENGTHENING THE BLACK COMMUNITY

To strengthen the Black Community, we need to strengthen those institutions and programs that are already doing good works. Institutions and programs that are necessary and we do not have, we need to create. Always, we must fight the enemy without and the enemy within at the same time, building constructive institutions and effective programs.

To strengthen the Black community, there are at least three areas that we must control or have the preponderance of influence over; from which I think the success of all other ventures, programs, and institutions flow. They are political, economic, and educational, not necessarily in that order, but surely in that package.

God Factor

I want to turn our attention elsewhere as the first priority; as the inescapable, absolutely necessary factor in strengthening our community. What is it? It is the God factor. As individuals and as a people, we must restore God to preeminence in our lives.

You can say this morning, I am an old man out of touch with reality. You can say, It's Sunday morning and he is a preacher—it's fairy tale time. Say what you please, but bear with me for a while. Let me present my case, and I shall ask God to put words in my mouth; and that which is dim, illuminate that to the height of every argument, I will be able to convincingly assert the preeminence of the Almighty, the presence of eternal providence.

I have thought long and hard about this matter, prayed night and day about it, argued continuously about it, and conversed incessantly about it. I am driven to the position that we need, must have, God back again at the center of our lives. And we must recapture a cultural emphasis. If we are going to strengthen our community and prosper in the future, in our homes, in our lives, in our communities, there must be God. And there must be culture. So many of our people are sick — physically, mentally, emotionally and spiritually. So many, many of our people are lost and confused. There is no spiritual center in their lives! No God reference. No African or cultural identity from which emanates ethics, morals, principles, respect, love, decency, family stability, community solidarity, and the cohesiveness of a people. Submission to the sovereignty of God and pride in our history is a kind of glue that holds things and people together.

Of all the statistics that trouble me most and reveal the depth of our ailments, internal violence, suicide, substance abuse, healthcare, and unwed mothers head the list. These are sins and weakness of the spirit; the absence of self-union to God and history, and they manifest themselves in the flesh where all can see. We make the mistake of looking for physical and programmatic solutions as the absolute cure, and so often we are left with frustration. Then despair sets in, for after putting forth our best effort, oftentimes little if anything is accomplished. The sickness prevails.

To make the point more graphic let us look at some statistics.

Homicide
Homicide has become a leading cause of death among urban Black men, who face a 1-in-10 chance of being killed, compared with a 1-in-80 chance for white men, according to congressional testimony.

For Black males ages 15 to 24, homicide is the leading cause of death; one of three Black men ages 20 to 24 is a homicide victim, according to the Institute for Advance Study of Black Family Life and Culture in Oakland, California.

Washington's record, 372 murders in 1988, shows that 351 of the victims were Black, and 235 of those (or 63 percent of the City's homicides) were males ages 15 to 34.

In New York City, in 1987, the latest period for which figures are available, 534 of the city's 1,672 murder victims were young Black males, according to the Crime Analysis Program at Boston's Northeastern University.

In Detroit, the figure was 352 of 686; in Los Angeles, 233 of 811.

Consider the Criminal Justice System

While African Americans account for 12 percent of the U.S. population, they account for 46 percent of the nation's prisoners. Nearly 9 of 10 Black inmates are men, and 54 percent of them are under 29 years of age.

Utilizing data from the Justice Department, a 1995 report by the Sentencing Project, a nonprofit organization that promotes alternative punishment and sentencing reform, states that 609,690 African Americans between ages 20 through 29 were in prison, in jail, or on probation or parole. In mid-1989, the figure represents 23 percent of the Black male population for that age group.

Significantly, it exceeds the number of Black men of all ages who were enrolled in college in 1986: roughly 436,000.

For white males in the same age category, 1,054,508 or 6.2 percent were incarcerated or on probation or parole. A total of 238,255 Latino males, or 10.4 percent, were in the criminal justice system.

A recent report from Washington, D.C. stated that 42 percent of Black males between 17 and 35 were involved with the criminal justice system. Twenty-one percent were on probation or parole, 15 percent were in jail, and 6 percent were being sought after.

Although fewer young women than men were in the system, there were still racial disparities: 164,249 whites, or 1 percent; 78,417 Blacks, or 2.7 percent, and 37,093 Latinos, or 1.8 percent.

Consider Unwed Mothers and Fathers
or Single-Parented Homes

There has been a dramatic increase in Black women heading households since 1960. The number of Black households headed by women has grown steadily. By 1988, almost 6 of 10 Black families with children under 18 were headed by single parents, and virtually all of those were women, according to the recent Census Bureau Report. About 2 in 10 comparable white families were headed by women.

In New York State, 50 percent of Black children and 42 percent of Latino children live with single parents, and almost exclusively that single parent is a woman. Sixty-one percent of Latino children and 41 percent of African American children live in households headed by someone with less than a high school education. Even though young Black males comprise 13 percent of the young male population, Black unwed fathers account for over 60 percent of all unwed fathers.

Consider Education

The news from the schools is not good. Enrollment of Black men in the nation's colleges dropped by 34,000 between 1976 and 1986, according to the American Council on Education. The percentage of Black men ages 18 to 24 in college dropped from 35.4 percent in 1976 to 27.8 percent in 1987, despite an increase in Black graduates from high schools with college-preparatory courses.

Between 50 percent and 60 percent of African American and Latino students do not graduate from high school. Forty-two percent of Black youths between ages 17 and 21 cannot read above the 6th-grade level.

Consider Healthcare

The state of healthcare of African Americans and Latinos is not good. According to health statistics for 1988, Black men suffered higher death rates from heart disease (68 percent higher than the total population), strokes (90 percent higher), cancer (71 percent higher), liver ailments (126 percent higher), and diabetes (86 percent higher). African Americans, mostly males, account for one in four cases nationwide of Acquired Immune Deficiency Syndrome.

The infant mortality rate is about 50 percent higher among Black babies than White babies. There is still a gap of about six years in life expectancy between African Americans and whites. White life expectancy is 75.4 years an increase from 75.3 years, while African American life expectancy has decreased from 69.7 years to 69.4 years, according to the National Center for Health Statistics.

And you have heard the report that Black males in Harlem have a lower life expectancy than men in Bangladesh.

Consider Poverty

Poverty is normal for multitudes of African Americans. In 1987, one in three Blacks was living below the poverty level, a number that has increased slightly since then, according to the Center on Budget and Policy Priorities, a Washington Research Group. The number of Black children under 18 living in poverty reached 45.6 percent in 1987, according to the center.

Northeastern University Center for Labor Market Studies found that the average real income for Black men ages 20 and 29 fell by 27.7 percent between 1973 and 1987, a deeper drop than the 17.8 percent decline seen by all men in the same age group.

In New York State, according to 1985 State and U.S. Census Projections, four out of ten Black children and five out of ten Latino children in the state live in families whose income is below the federal guidelines, which, as you know, is $10,989 in annual income for a family of four.

Consider Unemployment

The unemployment picture for African Americans is still bleak. The Urban League estimates that African Americans are unemployed at a rate of 2.2 times greater than that of whites. In a letter I received from the office of Congressman Thomas Bliley Jr., ranking Republican, containing excerpts from a speech he made before Congress, he writes,

> 40% of the 20-24 year old black male drop outs had no job in all of 1986, while the unemployment rate for white males was 4.0% in April 1989. The unemployment rate for black males was 10%. 38.8 % of black teenagers were unemployed compared to 12.3% of white teens.

When these statistics are studied, and for most of us, when these statistics take on flesh and blood, people we know, we don't have to be a genius to understand that something is terribly wrong with us. It cannot all be blamed on poverty and racism, as I will show presently. Nor will more and better programs and politics, answer all of our needs. But, we must never cease to work and struggle for more and better programs and politics.

I am convinced that our disintegration, produced over a long period of time by demonic racists, is deeper than material and /or natural answers and remedies can heal.

What Brought Us This Far?

After 400 years of unprecedented devastation, what brought us this far? What kept us together? What sustained us?

Remember those vicious racists who for hundreds of years went after the flower of the continent of Africa. They stole, and carted back to Europe, African art, African philosophy, African science, African theology—the physical manifestation of a people's spirit and mind. What they could not steal, they tried to destroy. African people must never know of their own magnificence. And then, employing every kind of evil means, they systematically inculcated the idea of African nothingness. African subhumanity, African ignorance; African dependence on Europeans; African hatred of Africa and Africans. And tragically, too many of our people accepted the idea and rejected themselves. In fact, they even went to war with themselves, and too many others went along to get along or stay alive.

And in the process, how many were physically killed? Twenty million? One-hundred million? To say nothing of the incalculable number killed mentally, emotionally, and spiritually, which may be the worst death of all.

We are not allowed to forget that Hitler killed 6 million Jews, although all the people killed during the Nazi nightmare were not Jews. But how many of us know or remember that the Belgians killed more Africans than that in the Congo? Twelve million is the estimate, and there are millions of other Africans, which no man can number. Who knows and who remembers and more importantly, who cares?

The end result of all that was the creation of a kind of self-hating Frankenstein monster, whose behavior was/is predictably anti-self and pro-European.

Just two references to underscore the depth of self-rejection. First, experiments still show that if you put a Black doll and a white doll before Black children and ask them to choose which is more beautiful and which one they would like to take care of and love, Black children inevitably reach for the white doll.

Second, Black religious people still make God white. They will spend millions of dollars to build massive cathedrals and depict God as white—to me, the most convincing evidence of self-rejection.

When one would make God—the symbol of the highest—in the image of those who have enslaved, subjugated, exploited, and humiliated them (and who are still doing so), it is unmistakable validation that they have despised themselves and internalized the superiority of Europeans or whiteness.

Malcolm X used to say, "The greatest crime the White man committed was teaching us to hate ourselves."

The sickness among us to which I have already alluded is the predictable manifestation of sustained inculcation over a long period of time — through institutions, movies, literature, tradition, history, mores, system, force terrorism, police, military, KKK., wealth, power, etc. — of the idea of superiority (the God-likeness) of Europeans and the inferiority (devil-likeness) of Africans.

Is it any wonder, I ask, that many of us are as negative and destructive as we are. We have been programmed to be against ourselves. And the only reason there is all this furor about so-called Black-on-Black crime or the pervasive Black criminality is that it threatens white people; it threatens the very fabric of society.

If it were confined among Black people, as it was intended, white folks would not give a damn. So let's be clear: Black criminality is directly related to European criminality. Europeans taught us to hate ourselves and influenced us to try to imitate their criminality.

Now, after saying all that, it becomes even more important to ask: What brought us this far? What kept us together? What sustained us in spite of all the evil that encircled and bombarded us?

What brought us through slavery? What held us together? What brought us through post-Reconstruction, when the hooded savages of the South, with the connivance of the hypocrites of the North, conspired to take back the small progress that was made during Reconstruction, one of the shining moments of American history? Every unmentionable terrorist tactic was employed. Every kind of treachery and betrayal was used to take back the meager gains; to beat, bomb, lynch, burn Black people out of existence, or into a state of impoverished servile submission.

What kept us together? What brought us through legal separation—called segregation—coming as it did with the *Plessy v.*

Ferguson decision of 1898. Segregation, an inhuman system designed to instill fear and self-hatred and to subject Black people to constant, daily humiliation and insults until the spirit was broken and the body and mind would go along with the program. African Americans were thus programmed to work against themselves. They were forced to drive pegs into their own hearts. What kept us together? What brought us this far?

Let's not forget the subtle *de facto* segregation of the rest of America — always, in less conspicuous ways than the South, but nonetheless just as real, just as humiliating. There were always reminders that Black people were considered inferior. What kept us together? What brought us this far?

Surely you would not argue that it was all due to our wisdom, genius, and perseverance. While we did have an abundance of those admirable qualities, and surely they helped, is that all? We did it by our own physical resources? No. We won't make that argument, for we know better. We know our physical resources, whatever they were, were no match against the power and might and the demonic forces that were arrayed against us.

No! The answer is elsewhere. The answer lies beyond the natural, beyond the rational. The answer is God. The mysterious other—who never left us, but kept us together, moving ahead—and giving an enslaved people a sense of our link to the motherland.

Our people gave God first place in their lives. They recognized that there was the Great Spirit, which did not leave them when they crossed the roaring waters. And this Great Spirit was prayed to, sung to, worshiped, and adored. And it was the glue that held them together; that kept them sane amid all the insanity.

This worship of God, the Great Spirit, provided a cosmology—an understanding of the universe; a theology and understanding of God in relation to their predicament; teleology—understanding of their purpose. When tied together, it gave them a place in the sun or in the universal order of things, even in the midst of slavery. It made them know that slavery and subjugation were not ordained for them. Their purpose, sanctioned by God, was to escape slavery and find freedom, where they could enjoy their God-given rights and develop their God-given potential. With this philosophy, this theology, they were able to carry on.

Faith and hope never left them. With an unshakable hope, inspired by God, they were able to celebrate hard times as they set it all to music. They affirmed the presence of God. "Up above my head, I hear music in the air. There must be a God somewhere."

With the slave master's whip in their ear, they could still sing, "Up above my head, I hear music in the air. There must be a God somewhere." They expressed hope of reaching a better city, a better country, a better time. "I've been tossed and driven, got no place to call my own, but I've been hearing of a city called heaven, and I'm trying to make it my home."

They sang of their determination to quit the horrors of slavery early. "I'm going home on the morning train, the evening train may be too late, so I'm going home on the morning train."

It is agreed that these songs also provided a code to convey messages to escape—plans, time and place of departure. But even so, at the center of it all was God. God was with them at work. When they gathered for various functions, God was with them; whether they planned to fight or escape or both, God was sovereign!

So through it all, slavery, post-Reconstruction, and segregation, God was revered and adored. But something happened. God was banished or relegated to last place or dismissed as irrelevant. And we are reaping the bitter harvest of our foolishness.

Back in the 70s, while White theologians were declaring the death of God amongst them, few of us suspected that God had died or been exiled from among us too.

When and why did this break occur? I think there were two periods: post-Reconstruction, which began about 1876, and the post Civil Rights era, which occurred between the late 60s and early 70s. During the post-Reconstruction era, the terrorist tactics of the racists did not encounter a church of resistance as during slavery. The black church was engaged in institutional maintenance, soul-purifying and heaven-going. Also whites were exerting influence over its worship style; traditional theology, if whites wanted to cool the fire of the church. They could never understand nor really feel a part of it. Yet they knew it played a significant role in the struggle of African people for liberation.

So the church lost some of its appeal. But still, God was very much the center of our people's life. The concentration of the church on its internal development was not sufficient reason for most Black people to turn away from God. It did, however, leave the field open for other organizations to take up the struggle of our people, which the church had monopolized. It was not until the mid-50s, when Dr. King came on the scene, that the church began to bestir itself and become an institution of resistance again.

By the time the early 70s had arrived, Black power was the expression of a deeper concept or idea or world view—nationalism, Black nationalism. The chief spokesperson was Malcolm X, a member of a Muslim group called the Nation of Islam. But there were other persons and movements and organizations, all of whom emphasized a strong connection to Africa. They changed their names, let their hair grow out, donned African apparel, talked African history, and emphasized the need for Black ownership of Black communities.

Christmas was replaced with Kwanzaa, although now, Dr. Karenga and others have argued that Kwanzaa was never created to replace Christmas. It was created as a (cultural) holiday for all African people. Be that as it may, the reality was, and to a significant degree is, that Kwanzaa was seen as replacing Christmas. After all, Christmas was about a White God who came to earth as a baby; moreover, Christmas was a season of exploitation, with its commercialization and Santa Claus.

Much of the criticism of Christmas was/is true. But the story of Christmas — God loving humanity so much that He came to earth to save humans, was born in a manger, grew up in poverty and experienced the usual human suffering, trouble, and betrayal, and finally was crucified — transcends culture and race. It is indeed the greatest story ever told. And at Christmas many parents would make a point of reading this story to their children, and it became part of their lives.

The reference to Christianity as the white man's religion showed the ignorance or deception of those who were pondering the idea. All so-called major Western religions, including Christianity, have an African origin.

Jesus Christ, according to the Bible, had African roots. The greatest theologians of the early church were Africans. Contrary to the popular notion, Europe was not the first to send missionaries to Africa. Africans sent missionaries to Europe. Europe came to Africa to study the Christian religion.

Just as their forefathers before them came to Africa to study philosophy, science, etc., and just as they came for cultural enrichment, the religion of Christianity attracted Europeans.

The monastery movement began in Africa—so Christianity is not the white man's religion; Europeans have merely *used* it, just as they have used other things of African creation.

Unfortunately, when this cultural assault was being waged against the church, the church, by-and-large, was not prepared to respond. There were a few people trying to argue the case for authentic Christianity. Dr. James Cone, in his book *Black Power, Black Theology,* tried to show the compatibility of Black power and Black theology; they go hand-in-hand.

Albert Cleague, with his Church of the Black Madonna, tried to incorporate Black nationalism into his theology and worship. There were a few others, Dr. Cornell West and Dr. Gayraud Wilmore. But the church really wasn't prepared for this cultural attachment upon its cherished beliefs and, as a result, great multitudes left the church.

Now the nationalists made two tragic mistakes, one already alluded to. They went to war with the church and, indirectly, with the God of the church, the God that had been the accepted deity of our people for hundreds of years, and this really wasn't necessary. The two could have walked together, complementing one another; all committed to the struggle for our people's realization of human rights and self-determination.

Today, to a significant degree, that is what is happening. But so much time and energy have been lost; so many lives have been wrecked and confused; and it need not have happened.

The second tragic mistake that the nationalists made was to cease the nationalist emphasis. After a few years passed, the nationalists' steam began to evaporate. People returned to their European ways. Three-piece suits and ties, straight hair and wigs for women, Jheri curls and perfectly cut hair for men until recently, when the hair took on all kinds of shapes and designs. There emerged a generation without history and culture; a generation that cannot relate to Black nationalism or Afrocentricity or the Christian Church. A generation without the blessing of either culture or Christ. This is the generation that is so sick.

Let me discuss here who else contributed to the break with

God. There was the radical revolutionary element. This element never had any love or respect for anybody's God. So when the nationalist went to war with the Christian God, they found eager allies in the radical/revolutionary element.

And finally, there was the contribution made by the petty bourgeoisie. This element was never the backbone of the Church, never contributed what it could have, but at least it claimed to be for the church.

But during this period in question, when the church needed their skills, talents, resources, they, for the most part, either paid lip service to the church or dismissed it as unnecessary or as the crutch of the weak and ignorant. At their worst, they joined the nationalist/radical/ revolutionary in attacking the church.

These were the forces at work against long-held Christian belief systems. When they were finished, God was banished from the lives of masses of people.

So here we are, 20, 25 years later, and the children of that time are largely responsible for the problems that engage us today. The parents of that time forsook the God of their fathers and mothers and therefore had no God to pass on, and this gave us offspring without God-consciousness or God-reference, without a sense of personhood and purpose; without a sense of responsibility to themselves and to family and community; without respect and decency.

This is the generation without an African connection, without cultural awareness—no Christ and no culture. This is the generation that can commit any crime without shame, inflict any pain for no reason, and have babies without concern, and use anything that promises a high. This is the generation without God-consciousness.

It should be pointed out in this connection that there were other factors at that time contributing to the confusion. The Vietnam war, with its violence, open use of drugs, free sex (or "free love" as they called it), and the disruption of families. There was a family in my church, a father and mother and two sons. The father was killed in Vietnam, the mother never recovered. She threw herself into death via the most destructive behavior. The sons today are a part of the problem. They are among the statistics I have cited.

Then there was Watergate. When those who were in the highest offices, who should have been models of honesty, who in fact were passing themselves off as such, were caught stealing, misusing funds, and obstructing justice, and the ring leader was the President of the United States who managed to escape through a pardon by his successor, President Gerald Ford.

There was the invasion of Grenada, and certainly the spiritual declension in white Christendom brought to its head by some theologians advocating "the death of God," had some influence, however marginal.

Surely all these contributed to the demonic forces that dethroned God and erased cultural awareness. And so for multitudes of African Americans, God died or was banished or was dismissed. And in homes and families where God's presence and sovereignty has always been acknowledged, there now existed a void or idols in the form of sex, songs, stimulants, and materialism took the throne of the Deity and children grew up without the God factor and without an African emphasis; with neither cosmic nor cultural connection.

Let me make the point with an illustration from the basketball court. One of the ways I try to stay in shape is by playing basketball. During the summer months I play in the park, usually Saturday morning and as many evenings as I can take. There are about three generations that play. There is the age group from 16 or 17 to late 20s. Then there is the 30 to 50 group. Then there are a few, very few, in the over 50 category. In fact, there is only one other person who may be near 50. So, at 60, I am in a class by myself. Now these games are hard fought. The competition is stiff. Some of these are former college players, and, in fact, some are still playing college ball, some are high school stars.

What adds to the competitiveness is that you have to win to stay on the court. Now there was this big fellow, call him John. John is about 6' 6" and 230 to 240, big bulging muscles and shiny Black skin — an imposing figure. One day John had an argument, a real shouting, threatening argument with another fellow, call him Jim. Jim was smaller than John, but Jim was always arguing and threatening people, and John didn't like him. So as the argument between the two heated up, I ran and got between them, pulling Jim away and returned to cool down John. John said to me, "I respect you, Rev., but I don't like that so and so." Later, as I stood on the sideline, he came to me and said, "Pardon me, Rev., I am from South Carolina. I grew up in the church." He then said, "I respect the church and the Rev." John came from a generation where God was still sovereign; where the church was important. So here he is many years later and a long way from home, but he has not forgotten. And when he is about to wreak havoc, which brings good to no one, you can stop him with reference to God. Just the presence or the symbol can stop him. He has a God-reference. He is no saint, but he has a God-reference.

Now, the other generation, the generation following John's, curse all day, up and down the court, and never say excuse me, or pardon me, or show any indication of shame at all.

Several weeks ago I spoke at a youth retreat to a group of about 200, ranging in age from 16 to 21. My wife and I were invited to spend four days with them. Near the end of the retreat, they had a session on male/female relationships. They were very honest, apparently, and very open. They mostly talked about sex. What shocked me was that having sex was a foregone conclusion; at issue was sleeping around. At no point was there mentioned, even for discussion sake, sex only after marriage. Now I am not naive nor am I a prude, but I would think that somebody would raise the question. Somebody would discuss virginity and marriage. But not a soul. Do we wonder why there is such a proliferation of unwed mothers and fathers? Do we, in our families, in our churches, hold forth as a standard to be emulated the sanctity of marriage and sex and love and marriage?

There must be standards even if we don't reach them. St. Paul once said, "Let God be true even if every man is a liar." If we are going to strengthen our communities, we must set some standard! We must have a moral code. We have to have values as it relates to humanity, to work, to struggle, to family, to community. We must repair the old landmark.

It was said that the mighty Roman Empire fell because the gods become common. What the observer had reference to was the practice of the Romans to have the statue of the gods beside them in their pursuit of pleasure. In their minds all that humans were doing, the gods would be doing with them. So the gods were no different from humans.

So Rome no longer had a symbol that could hold it together. The highest had been brought down to the lowest. There were no values, no morals left, so Rome fell. And so will fall all nations and peoples and persons who forget God or banish God or reduce God to the common drives of the flesh.

Let us strengthen the Black communities by repairing the old landmark; raise the altar again, the altar dedicated to the worship of God.

Let us put altars in our homes. I am not saying take the bars out, although it would not hurt to do that. I am saying put an altar *in*, and make it a practice to gather there with the family.

God says to us, If my people who are called by my name will humble themselves and pray, and seek my face and turn from their wicked ways, I will hear from heaven, forgive their sins and heal their land.

If *my* people; never mind about the other people.

If my people will humble themselves, pray and seek my face, turn from their wickedness, I will hear, forgive, and heal.

There is still time. Let's repair the old landmark.

Let us start praying again as individuals, as families. Let us begin fasting again. It is a good exercise for both physical health and spiritual health.

Let us take out the Bible again. Let us read for ourselves and to our children. These old Bible stories will help shape their lives.

And let us go back to our history book again. To African history. Let us teach ourselves, our children, and our communities about the greatness of our history: How we created the earliest civilizations in the Nile Valley, in Kemit called Egypt, where we studied and developed religion, art, and philosophy — where we studied the movement of the heavenly bodies, where we studied medicine hundreds of years before Hippocrates who came to be called the father of medicine after Imhotep had already diagnosed and treated over 200 diseases.

The Greeks knew about Africa, for they stole from the Egyptian's mystery system the knowledge they later claimed as their own. Aristotle must bear the dubious distinction of being the biggest academic thief in history.

Let us teach how we raised pyramids—which still boggle the mind — from the dust of Egypt.

Let us teach how we created civilizations, not only in Egypt, but in the Indus Valley, in India, from which come the Black God, Buddha; and the Sumerian civilization between the Tigris and Euphrates Rivers, where Babylon with its high walls and hanging gardens became a wonder of the world and whose builder was Black Nimrod, according to the Bible.

Let us teach how we built civilizations on the west coast of Africa: Mali, Songhay, with their great builders and warriors, Mansa Musa and Sundiata.

Let us teach how even in Spain we created the most advanced society, where we ruled for seven hundred years.

Yes, let us teach how we navigated the great waterways of the world. Teach how we arrived in America long before Columbus discovered he was lost.

Let us teach how we reared huge buildings from the earth, hammered out roads and highways, smelted metals for various usages, wrote great literature, drew exquisite pictures, carved and shaped magnificent works of art, composed great music.

Let us teach how we philosophized and theologized, how we developed complex theological and philosophical systems.

Let us teach how we once conceived and implemented elaborate forms of governments with structures of jurisprudence, economy, industry, and commerce.

Let us teach how we created great educational systems, how our families were intact, securely wrapped in traditions based upon thousands of years of experiment, how we were kind to each other, protected each other, and loved each other.

Let us teach how African people were once the marvels of the world. All other people wanted to be like Africans. Europe came to Africa to become civilized, for cultural enrichment.

Let us teach how we built this country, how Black slave labor and freedmen's labor built this country; how our labor and our bodies, which were bartered in the slave trade, built the wealth of white Western civilization.

So with our Bible in one hand, our history books in the other hand; with God at the center of our spirit, and our history at the center of our minds; with cosmic citizenship and cultural credentials, we will be able to launch a spiritual and cultural revolution. And while working ceaselessly to support and create programs and institutions of uplift and enhancement, we will be able to build our communities into places of beauty, peace, love, and prosperity.

Let us go back to church regularly, and let us give generously of our time, talent, and treasure.

Let us give God sovereignty over our lives.

If we do that, I am convinced, our communities will come alive. We as a people will prosper with love and respect for one another. Our elders will be revered, our children will be loved and protected, our young people will be admired, and our family will be stable — a home will be a place of peace, happiness, and love.

Yes, we as a people will make it to the Promised Land.

FROM VICTIMS TO VICTORS—
RESPONDING CREATIVELY
TO CHANGE IN THE CITY

The subject which I have been invited to address—"From Victims to Victors, Responding Creatively to Change in the City"—demands that we first define the who, the what and the how of victimization. *Webster's Dictionary* defines "victims" as : "a living being sacrificed to a deity or in the performance of a religious rite; or one that is acted on and usually adversely affected by a force or agent; one that is injured, destroyed, or sacrificed under any of various conditions; one that is subjected to oppression, hardship, or mistreatment; one that is tricked or duped."

Who are the Victims?

No matter which of the definitions we select from the above, the essential characteristic of victimization is that the victim is at the mercy of forces, or systems or people. Victims are generally the excluded. They are what the Bible calls "aliens," "outsiders," the "least of these." They are all nationalities, colors, genders and sexual orientations.

However, there are whole nationalities or ethnic groups that bear the stamp of "victims." As a particular race or ethnic group, or religion they have been exploited, enslaved, colonized, and oppressed by other people, races, or nationalities, precisely because of their nationality and/or religion. And within that oppressed nationality, there can be and usually is victimization. The victims victimizing the victim is a kind of double victimization produced by members of the victim's own victimized people. Black-on-Black crime is a conspicuous example.

One should not should think this process strange, for inherent in victimization is the eradication of loyalty and commitment to the advancement of the victim's people. Moreover, the self-rejection instilled in the victim produces self-hatred that manifest itself in rejection of and violence against the victim's own people.

It follows that those who are the victimizers, and obviously if there are victims, there must be victimizers—exploiters, oppressors, enslavers, colonizers—who, more often than not, in their quest for power, wealth, and /or privilege will victimize or oppress or dehumanize their own people.

In southern U.S.A., in particular, poor whites were victimized by whites who exploited both black and white. But, whites, however, impoverished and exploited could still enjoy the satisfaction of knowing they were better than the "nigger," "nigra" or colored. So, Blacks took on a passive, turn-the-other-cheek, accommodating Jesus Christ; whites took on a cruel, dehumanizing segregating Jim Crow posture.

Those in power or the victimizers, also engineer distance and conflict between or among victimized groups. I remember saying to a Jewish woman on a TV program, as we discussed Black/Jewish relationships, "The scapegoat is made to scapegoat the scapegoat."

Another interesting characteristic of the victim or victims is that they will blame themselves for their own victimization. This they do because those who have victimized them have convinced them after all, the victimizers have the propaganda machinery backed up by powerful and authoritative institutions and systems—that they, the victims, are totally responsible for their own behavior and condition. The victimizers create the victims or condition or forces, which create, or at least help to create, the victims—then blame the victim for being a victim. It is as though Dr. Frankenstein blamed his creation for being a monster.

Those of us of African ancestry believe we have been victimized more than any other people. Now, I know there are others who would vie for the dubious distinction as the world's number one sufferer or victim. Some years ago, I was a member of a delegation that visited the German Democratic Republic. The delegation comprised of a Jew, a Chicano, a Native American and a Puerto Rican. After we had visited the Sachenhousen Concentration Camp, and the Death Memorial in Schewen, in North Germany, where Hitler had decided to march Jews into the sea, we got to discussing who had suffered the most. I kind of think I won the debate—a debate I wish I hadn't won . . . I wish there had never been such a topic to provoke a debate.

So being an expert on victimization, born of experience and information, let me briefly share with you how enslavers, colonizers, exploiters, oppressors have created and/or sustained the victimization, oppression, or dehumanization of people of African ancestry through the implementation of a process or a series of actions/strategies I call NED. The Transliteration for NED is negation emasculation and decimation.

Negation is a series of actions in which the victim is negated or denied existence. The "invisible man," is what Ralph Ellison called it in his book by the same title. "Nobody know my name," cried James Baldwin. When I grew up there was no such thing as African history. Africa never contributed anything. In fact, there was seldom any mention of the continent of Africa. This great, big, old continent, 2 ½ times the size of the U.S.A. was just not important. And, when there was a reference, it was in the most disparaging terms.

The process of emasculation rids the victim of humanity. It strips away every shred of humanness. Negation denies the existence of the victim. Emasculation acknowledges the victims and attempt to reduce the victim to nothingness. In the Dred Scott decision, Chief Justice Taney stated "Black people have no rights that White people are bound to respect." To deny a person access to the job market or opportunities for entrepreneurial efforts, to deny social mobility, education, and to create distorted, disparaging images of a person, is to emasculate that person. When the person, or victim resists negation and /or emasculation, then the victimizers employ methods that lead to the victims's destruction or decimation.

Now, if you want to spiritualize victimization, we can say that it is the devil who has victimized the victims, and we would be on solid biblical ground. Paul said: "We wrestle not against flesh and blood, but against principalities and powers, the rulers of this world of darkness, the evil spirits and regions above." However we want to view the ultimate cause, the end result for the victim is the same, a denial of rights and opportunities. If a person does not have food, shelter, and raiment, what does it matter to him or her whether there is some invisible, supernatural agent, called the devil, or some visible, natural agents called people who have created his or her condition.

In addition, what this means is that our struggle must be both spiritual and natural. Or to put it another way, for those of us who are Christians, we believe with Paul that behind the seen evil there are unseen forces at work. We must always prioritize spiritual weapons; ceaseless prayer, frequent fasting, worship, meditation, constant Bible and devotional literature study. We must do these things even as we use the weapons of this world.

When Joshua stood at the bank of the Jordan River, ready to lead the people of God into the Promised Land, there were mighty enemies and many obstacles that awaited them. The instructions God gave Joshua did not address the enemies or the obstacles, but Joshua's own mental and spiritual readiness.

> My servant Moses is dead. So, prepare to cross the Jordan River with all the people into the land I will give the Israelites. As I promised Moses, I will deliver to you every place where you set your foot. Your domain is to be all the lands of the Hittites, from the desert and from Lebanon east to the great River Euphrates and west to the great sea. No one can withstand you while you live. I will be with you as I was with Moses. I will not leave you nor forsake you. Be firm and steadfast, so that you may give this people possession of the land which I swore to the fathers I would give them. Above all, be firm and steadfast, taking care to observe the entire law which my servant Moses enjoined on you. Do not swerve from it either to the right or to the left that you many succeed wherever you go. Keep this book of the law on your lips. Recite it by day and by night, that you may observe carefully all that is written in it, then you will successfully attain your goal. I command you: Be firm and steadfast! Do not fear nor be dismayed, for the Lord, your God, is with you wherever you go. (Joshua 1:1-9)

Redefinition of Reality

Now that we have observed the who, what, and how of victimization, we can now discuss moving the victim to victors. In that process, the victims must redefine reality, starting with themselves. An aspect of power is to define reality on its terms and to force acceptance on the rest of the world. Obviously, how the powerful define reality is in their own interest, and that interest is to stay in power.

If the victims are going to be the victors, a redefinition is imperative. The victims must contest the victimizers' stance. As long as the victims believe they are helpless victims, there is no help! Not even from God. In the story we have read from scripture, when the spies returned from their mission, they agreed that the promise of the beauty and bountifulness of the land that they were to possess was true. But, they said the people were giants, the walls of the city touched heaven, and they were grasshoppers in their eyes and grasshoppers in the eyes of their adversaries. These men, not many years removed from the bondage of Egypt, still had a slave mentality. They still suffered from their victimization in Egypt. There they were, having been delivered miraculously, having seen one marvelous event after another on their behalf, and still they were unable to divest themselves of their plantation mentality. They were hopeless victims.

In a crucial moment, in which the direction of history awaited their decision, in that moment, they let the secret out, they viewed themselves as grasshoppers. And, then, the inevitable, they projected their grasshopper ism upon their enemies. They said, they think we are grasshoppers too. Then another instructive development. These victims, with their grasshopper mentality, blamed Moses! They said that he had brought them and their children out of Egypt to die in the wilderness. The strange and peculiar perceptions and actions of victims.

But God, who had by now lost His patience, said: "You will die in the wilderness and your children, who you said would die in the wilderness, shall enter the Promised Land. A grasshopper mentality can never inherit the future. (Numbers 13:33)

Victims with a mindset firmly fixed in the victim syndrome will never be victors. They can never respond creatively to change in the city. They can never respond creatively to anything. They will die in the wilderness of fear, of failure, of untapped potential, and self-rejection.

On the other hand, when victims rethink their victimization, re-define themselves—particularly with reference to their cosmic citizenship, their relationship with God—they are on the road to becoming a victor. It is the reason history, an accurate reading of history, is so important. I know this to be true where people of African ancestry are concerned. An accurate understanding of history is a potent tool in a redefinition of reality. But, as important as history and a definition grounded in history and culture are, they are nothing compared with a definition that can boast a reference to God and redemption. A definition that declares: Yes, I am special! Beyond all that, the God who redeemed me tells me I am special!

When the apostle Paul's credentials were questioned, he validated his authenticity by first pointing to his impeccable cultural credentials.

> Though I might also have confidence in the flesh. If any other man thinketh that he hath whereof he might trust in the flesh, I more: Circumcised the eighth day, of the stock of Israel, of the tribe of Benjamin, an Hebrew of the Hebrews; as touching the law, a Pharisee; Concerning zeal, persecuting the church; touching the righteousness which is in the law, blameless. (Philippians 3: 4-6)

Then, he went on to say:

> But what things were gain to me, those I counted loss for Christ. Yea doubtless, and I count all things but loss for the excellency of the knowledge of Christ Jesus my Lord: for whom I have suffered the loss of all things, and do count them but dung, that I may win Christ. And be found in him, not having mine own righteousness, which is of the law, but that which is through the faith of Christ, the righteousness which is of God by faith. (Philippians 3: 7-9)

Significantly, it is worth noting that Paul came to this exalted conclusion after he had discussed his history and culture. There are those who want to dismiss history and culture before they have understood their importance. In other words, if the victims can bring themselves to declare their somebodiness, their uniqueness, with reference to history, culture, and redemption, then they will be able to say, with Peter, We have been redeemed not with corruptible things, like silver and gold, but with the precious Blood of Jesus Christ. God has placed such value upon us that He has allowed His Son to die for us. If the victims redefine themselves with these references, inexorably the victims will become the victors.

Again, when the spies returned with the majority report, unshakable in the opinion that they were victims, that they were grasshoppers, they were helpless. There was a minority report brought by Joshua and Caleb, and they were as unshakable in their faith as the others were in their doubt. They said, God is with us, we can take the land. God responded to their audacious faith, by making them leaders who would take the next generation to victory.

Redefinition of the Victimizers

When the victims redefine themselves they force the oppressor or the victimizers to redefine themselves. In this struggle for definitions, a startling discovery is made by the victims. The victimizers are not as powerful as they appear to be. There is an illusionary quality about power. It is seldom what it seems to be. It is fragile and transitory, and whoever has it, should wear it like a loose garment.

Now, when the Israelites sent spies again forty years after the first occurence, they entered Jericho and discovered that the people had known of the mighty works that God had done on behalf of the Israelites, how He had brought them from victims to victors, and they trembled in fear. The power that the Israelite spies thought these people had forty years before was nonexistent. The people they feared, feared them. One group of people, on the outside of the wall trembling with fear, and the other people on the inside of the wall trembling with fear. (See Joshua 2:1-14)

Elusiveness of Victimizers

In this struggle for definition, it is necessary to unmask the victimizer, and this is not an easy task. They are society's model citizens. They occupy the highest pinnacles of power, and wealth and privilege. They are bankers and financiers, politicians, educators, artists, Christians, Jews, Muslims, they contribute to worthy causes. The primary reason they are elusive is that they have created or inherited systems, institutions, traditions, and mores that do the victimizing for them. Moreover, unwittingly the innocent are drawn into the matrix. They share the spoils of the exploitation.

The great sin of this innocent crowd is that they want to maintain their ignorance. They want to pretend that they are not the beneficiaries of these unjust arrangements, or they remain silent. I think it was John Burke who said, "All that is necessary for evil to triumph is that good people remain silent." Dr. King said during the struggle in Birmingham that the great evil of Birmingham was not what bad people did, but that good people did nothing.

Victims' Appreciation of Their Own Resources

Having completed the definition exercise, the victim must move next to the analysis, understanding, and appreciation of their own talents, abilities, and resources. Once the victims have come to see themselves in a new light, they will view their abilities—what they can do—and their resources in a different way. What they will discover is that they have enormous abilities and resources. It has been said that Black wealth is the ninth largest nation in the world. Yet there are more than nine hundred thousand eligible, unregistered Black voters in New York State. It has been said that if all eligible Blacks had voted according to their numbers in ten states, Dukakis would have been elected president in 1988. If a substantial portion of Black economic and political power were utilized, there would be a major difference in America, indeed in the world. Victims have gifts and resources. The challenge is to convince the victims of that fact.

Victims' Search for Allies

Now, the victims, having redefined themselves, and the victimizers, having located and analyzed their resources, must take us to the third step in moving toward victor-allies. Victims must have allies. We have emphasized the necessity of self-definition, understanding, and appreciation of one's own history, culture, abilities, and resources. This alone will bring significant change to the victims and their condition. But, if the victims are going to reach their full potential and radically alter their condition, there must be allies.

An essential part of the victims' growth is the ability to live and work with others. First, begin with their own people and then move outward. If there are those who may be irritated by attention or emphasis being placed on the victims' love of self and love of their own people, let us remember that Jesus early on confined Himself primarily to His own people, telling His disciples to go first to the lost tribes of Israel. Later, Jesus said, "Go into all the world and preach the Gospel to all creatures." And as He was about to enter into heaven, He promised His disciples that they would receive the Holy Ghost, after which they would be witnesses for him in Jerusalem, Judea, and Samaria and to the uttermost parts of the world. Again, notice the order. They were to start at home first. The great Jewish Rabbi Hillel once said, "If I am not for myself, who will be for me? If I am only for myself, what am I? If not now, when?"

Logically, the natural place for victims to find allies would be among other victims. There are many things in which victims share. While there are differences and peculiarities, still there is much victims have in common. But coalescing with victims is not an easy task. For reasons already discussed, victims are taught to be fragmented, internally and externally.

Ideally, a coalition of victims and those powerful and wealthy supporters who have come to identify with the victims is a consummation devoutly to be wished. It was this kind of coalition Dr. King had put together. In the Poor People's campaign, the objective was to achieve economic, political, and social justice for all Americans and the strategy was to bring thousands of people to Washington, D.C., and not to return home in the evening as had been done in 1963. But, this time to stay in Washington and to tie up everything there until the promise had been delivered. What a creative way to bring change! Dr. King never completed the task. He was killed on April 4, 1968.

The inevitable question is: What is the role of those who have either achieved or been born to power, wealth, and privilege? What is the role of the members of the dominant class or race? What is the role of those who are reaping benefits from the status quo?

What benefits are derived at the expense of the poor, the exploited, and the oppressed? What is their role in helping victims become victors? It is an old question, which has been answered before and the answer has not changed.

1. *Identify with the victims.* Become one with the victims. Internalize the pain of the victims. Jesus Himself is our example. He came to earth, took on humanity, was in all points tested as we are, yet He remained without sin.

2. *Provide resources.* Once the identification or empathy question is settled, resources should be provided. Resources in terms of money, expertise, physical space, etc.

3. *Converting victimizers.* Another important way the victims can be helped is in converting the creators and/or keepers and/or beneficiaries of the status quo. Much of the victims' problems would be eliminated if the victimizers were converted or changed.

The Kerner Commission in 1967 stated that the ghetto was the creation of white society. If that is true, then greater emphasis must be placed on the conversion of the creators and/or sustainers of the ghetto. If missionaries could have converted the white slave masters and colonizers and left Africa and the other lands alone to continue their own development, which in most things were far in advance of Europe, the world might be a better place for all peoples.

Why should anyone believe that the Gospel of Jesus Christ would not have reached into the interior of Africa, coming from northern and eastern Africa, where it had taken root long before it had been established in Europe? There is evidence that Europe came to Africa, not only for cultural enrichment, but for religious conversion and enlightenment.

Why should anyone believe that given Europe's history of barbarism, exploitation, and oppression, they had been singled out by the almighty to bring the Gospel of peace, brotherhood, and sisterhood, of redemption and of abundance to Africa in particular, but also to other peoples? How can anyone believe such a thing, without the affliction of the old disease of racism and an illusion of supremacy and superiority?

It is not difficult to understand why this mission to the victimizers and beneficiaries of exploitive systems is neglected or dismissed in favor of a mission to the victims. It is easier, more romantic and more praiseworthy and material gaining. It is easier to convert the criminals in the streets than the criminal in the suites. It is easier and more exciting to attempt to change the thieves in the slums than the thieves in suburbia and the savings loan association bandits.

It is easier to change the crooks and manipulators on the inner city mean streets than the crooks and manipulators on Wall Street. It is easier and more exciting and more praiseworthy, and more ego-satisfying to go ten thousand miles to convert blacks in Africa than to convert whites in the U.S.A. and Europe.

Let it be clearly understood, help that does not intend to make the victim independent, yes, even of the helpers, is nothing more than a subtle attempt—conscious or unconscious—by the helpers to sustain the status quo, while at the same time massaging their egos. There is an old proverb that goes: Give a person a fish and you have satisfied his hunger for a moment. And you will have to give him a fish the next day and the next and the next. But teach him to fish, and he will be able to feed himself.

Responding Creatively

The second phase of our topic—responding creatively to change in the city—must be approached with great reluctance. My own experience and my understanding of the strange ways God works in the Bible, makes me reluctant to lay out a plan of action in advance. I know there needs to be a strategy, a method, prior research and thought. I know there needs to be a plan. I know the saying: Those who fail to plan, plan to fail. And I know this from a personal point of view.

Oh, I could tell about the Lily Foundation's many programs to assist churches in creatively responding to the needs of housing, economic development, training and teaching church leaders. I could inform you about the training or courses now being prepared by New York Theological Seminary, New York Mission Society and the Dinkins' Administration.

I could tell you about my own direct involvement as the chairperson of the African American Clergy and Elected Officials, which convenes all the Black elected officials in Brooklyn and a significant number of clergy. As chairperson of the Association of Brooklyn Clergy for Community Development, an ecumenical group of 50 churches, we have in the last two years co-sponsored 58 new two-family affordable housing units and will complete 130 of the same by October 1993. We have renovated 30 units and will complete 93 by next year. We have one of the largest and most effective AIDS programs in the city. We have an experimental program for emotionally disturbed youngsters, where we place them in a residential setting rather than in institution. I could talk to you about our after-school programs, senior citizens and substance abuse programs, our coalition work, bringing minority business people together with city officials to secure equitable opportunities.

And I could speak of my own church's attempt to respond creatively to the change in the city. Our youth programs are mentoring programs—which include "Man to man and Sister to sister"; Kush Cultural Center, where children meet on Saturdays for cultural educational and recreational enhancement; our Day Care Center for children ages two to five and our high schools and college student achievement programs that assist students in achieving excellence. I could talk about our Rescue, Redirect and Prevention Program for youth in trouble with the law, our AIDS education and prevention program for youth, Stop the Violence Program with parents of the victims of violence.

I could talk to you about our Timbuktu Learning Center, co-sponsored by Medgar Evers College, which includes a Monday night study group dealing with relevant issues in the context of history. The Tuesday night lecture series that convenes some of the most renown scholars, diplomats, activists to share their knowledge and experience with the community. Wednesday nights the Religious Institute holds bible study classes as well as classes with an Afrocentric focus. Furthermore, I could speak to you regarding our outreach ministries designed to reach individuals with the Gospel of Jesus Christ: street ministry, door to door, home Bible study, evangelistic meetings, etc.

At the base of all these programs, the driving force is Jesus Christ. It is not always stated explicitly, but He is always there. We are what we are because of Him. And, what we are will manifest itself in all that we do and say. Even in our demonstrations, marches rallies, boycotts, the presence of Christ is very real to us. Some of our strongest members come by way of demonstration. That is why it is not always easy to know when an action is social or spiritual. I have prayed for the sick, and the sick were not healed. I have preached individual salvation and none was saved. I have pleaded for church members, and nobody joined. On the other hand, I have led demonstration in the fight for justice, and people followed me back to the church, gave their lives to Jesus Christ and are some of our strongest members today.

How shall we respond creatively to change in the city? With faith! Surely, constantly analyzing all methods and ideas, ever ready to experiment, but knowing that our ways are not God's ways. A particular ministry for one person or church may not be for another person or church. At bottom, our faith is the one never wavering, never changing factor.

Faith

What is key, what is of paramount importance, what must be deeply impressed upon the converted or changed victim and the victim's allies is that God is still in charge. And change, victory, "comes not by power, nor by might, but by my Spirit saith the Lord." And that God demands of those who follow Him, or of those who would bring freedom, justice, and peace, of those who would work for a world where all people live together as family, and enjoy the prosperity of this abundant earth, of those who would bring salvation and healing—God demands of these, faith! Faith for salvation and a faith in God's methodology.

We must leave God "free to act" on the spur of the moment. We must leave the future open, and always be ready to go with God wherever He leads. It may be that God will say to us, as He said to Abraham, leave all and I will show you a land you will afterward inherit. And the Bible said: "He went out not knowing where he went."

When Moses wanted a blueprint, God said, Go and I will go with you. When they shall ask who sent you, say *I am that I am.* Do not underestimate faith. It is, someone has said, a stick of dynamite in an unjust system. It is subversive to say to the victim, you can be a victor. You can change things. Have faith in God.

CHAPTER FOUR

PART I
WHAT WOULD JESUS CHRIST DO?

PART II
THE ORIGIN OF JESUS CHRIST

PART III
SEARCH FOR A REVOLUTIONARY JESUS
FOR A REVOLUTIONARY AGE

PART IV
JESUS, THE SURPRISING CONTEMPORARY

WHAT WOULD JESUS DO?

Back in 1937, Charles M. Sheldon wrote a book entitled, *In His Steps*.[1] The substance of the book centered on the question, "What would Jesus do?," and on its impact on people who attempted to answer this question in terms of their daily lifestyles. The book became a best seller. While this is a legitimate question, of paramount importance for any individual or people at any time, it is even more so for people of African descent in the U.S.A.

Moreover, just as it is important that we study deeply Jesus' life and ponder life's challenges with reference to the question, "What would Jesus do?," it is equally important that we ask who Jesus was in a historical context. For Blacks, the question is crucial. The Europeanization of Christianity has alienated innumerable Blacks, for the same Europeans who gave us the Bible also took everything from us.

The history of Black people is unlike the history of any other people. The peculiar nature of European and American savagery to which Black people have been subjected significantly reduced a once-proud people who had created civilization to a rootless, self-loathing, powerless herd.

The enslavement of Black people was more than slavery of the physical person. Europeans and Americans went for the soul of Africa. It was not enough to steal and pollute and corrupt the persons. Europeans wanted more. They craved the essence of African humanity and therefore stole and/or distorted history itself, so that Blacks were thrust into the void. They carted back to Europe African art, literature, and philosophy and claimed it all for themselves, all the while proclaiming Africa's lack of civilization.

A classic example of this thievery is that of Egyptian Mystery School philosophy. This academic thievery is documented in George G.M. James' book *Stolen Legacy*.[2]

What Europeans could not steal or distort, they destroyed. Africans must never know of their past greatness. They must be forced to internalize the superiority of Europeans, thus rejecting themselves and embracing European enemies.

Jews and their allies constantly remind us of their experience at the hands of Aryans, especially as it relates to Hitler. Every schoolboy knows that Hitler killed six million Jews. In New York, now there is even talk about building a monument with the taxpayer's money to remember their holocaust.

But who recounts the tales of horror visited upon *our* forebears? How many Africans were killed in the slave trade alone? A hundred million? Four hundred million? Malcolm X used to make reference to Dwight Lowell Dumond's book on slavery, where Professor Dumond says one hundred million Africans were uprooted from their homeland. Yet at the end of slavery there were not twenty-five million Africans in the western hemisphere.[3] "What happened to the 75 million?," Malcolm would ask in his inimitable fashion and he would go on to say, "Their bodies are at the bottom of the ocean and their blood and their bones have fertilized the soil of this country...." Who will tell *our* story? Who will rear a monument to *our* holocaust?

Every race has benefitted from our degradation. Like vultures, they have feasted on our carcasses. We have been enslaved, exploited, dehumanized as no other people. This is why to speak of Black-on-Black crime without relating it to the worldwide criminal behavior of Caucasians is nonsense. Caucasians have created the conditions that make the internecine struggle among Blacks inevitable.

Physical slavery merged into colonialism and then neocolonialism, the last stage of imperialism, as Kwame Nkrumah called it. Walter Rodney, in his monumental book *How Europe Underdeveloped Africa*, demonstrates how Europe was able to capture and control African land and resources.[4]

Even at this late date in history, colonialism and neocolonialism are not dead, neither at home nor abroad. Feeding this slave-making, colonial, neocolonial monster, hovering over it, protecting it, was and is the Europeanization of Christianity. The fact that white Christians helped to create and benefitted from this whole saga is indisputable. It was Bishop LasCasas who urged the importation of Black slaves into the New World in 1517.[5] John Hope Franklin writes:

> Finally, this was the period in which Europeans developed a rationalization for their deeds based on Christianity. The Portugese and the Spaniards led Europeans in invoking the missionary zeal of Christianity to justify their activities on the African coast. If they were chaining Negroes together for the purpose of consigning them to a lifetime of enforced servitude, it was "a holy cause" in which they had the blessings of both their king and their church.[6]

Missionaries who went to Africa did not appreciate Africans as human beings with a rich history. Instead, they saw a bunch of savages waiting for European enlightenment. They identified with colonial governments and helped to soften and adjust Africans to the European order of things. There is a lot of truth in the saying: Before the Europeans came, we had the land and they had the Bible. Now Europeans have the land and we have the Bible. In his book *African Glory*, J. C. DeGraft-Johnson quotes a couple of missionaries who are representative of the missionary mentality (as reported by Lothrop Stoddard in his *The Rising Tide of Colour*):

> Fortunately the white man has every reason for keeping a firm hold on Africa. Not only are its central tropics prime sources of raw materials and foodstuffs which white direction can alone develop, but to north and south the white man has struck deep roots into the soil. Both extremities of the continent are "white man's country" where strong white peoples should ultimately arise. Two of the chief white powers, Britain and France, are pledged to the hilt in this racial task and will spare no effort to safeguard the heritage of their pioneering children . . . .[7]

He also quotes Henri Junod from *Ba Ranga*:

> I speak of resignation. It is necessary to the Blacks, for despite all that has been written on the fundamental axiom of the absolute equality of mankind, they are an inferior race, a race made to serve.[8]

Moreover, when Africans began their gallant fight for independence, not many white Christians supported them. After years of violent exploitation and oppression by Europeans, even the mildest form of protest — far before it had reached the violent stage — was denounced. White Christians could not bring themselves to support their Black fellow-believers in their quest for human dignity. Sadly, not all Blacks supported liberation ventures either, since they had deeply internalized everything Europeans had designed for them. European violence and subjugation were accepted while the feeblest acts of violence to counteract European violence was condemned.

So completely had Christianity become associated with Europeans that all Christian religious artwork portrayed European likenesses. All the good guys, including God, were white. All the bad guys, including the devil, were Black. The English language — in the hands of white Christians and some blacks ones as well — became the enemy of Blacks.

"Black Judas, yeah, Black Judas!" screamed the narrator in the play *Black Nativity*. Without being told, we would have known that Judas would be played by a Black man, and Jesus Christ would be portrayed by the whitest of white men in the movie version of "Jesus Christ Superstar."

White Christians taught Blacks to sing, "Make Me Whiter Than Snow, Lord." One could readily understand how whites were carried along with this deception—after all, it must have been extremely satisfying for their starved egos. But how could Black people not only accept this arrangement, but joyfully participate in their own degradation and vigorously defend their actions against all questioners?

The disintegration of the African identity was so complete that Blacks now made God in the likeness of their white oppressor, and fell down and worshiped this white image. It followed that even without physical chains, Blacks were still enslaved and would behave subserviently in all areas of mind and action before whites. Even the Bible was brought in to undergird the legitimacy of white oppression of Blacks. Did not Noah curse Black Ham to be a servant to his brothers? Did not Paul teach servants to obey their masters?

Thus, the life of Black humanity was encircled and sucked dry by Europeans' economic, political, social, and pre-eminently religious systems, which they had stolen and twisted until they shaped them in their own likeness and promoted their own interest, which was to rule the world.

Is it any wonder then that many, when brought face-to-face with this reality, became vehemently anti-Christian. To them, Christianity was "the white man's thing"— or "trick bag"— created to enslave Blacks, persuading them to adjust to their own subjugation. Others echoed Karl Marx's contention that religion was the opiate of the people, which promised pie in the sky, by and by, while the capitalists got their pie now; and still others did not think it even worthwhile for debate.

Significantly, one of the periods of the church's finest hours was also the period of its traumatic break with Blacks. The Civil Rights Movement involved many Christians in the struggle. But it was too little too late and when substantial change was not forthcoming, it marked the end of the wholesale acceptance of Christianity for Black Americans.

In the sultry Alabama sun, back in 1966, Stokely Carmichael gave vent to the frustration, discontent, and hope of millions of Blacks. "Black Power!" he shouted, and with that we took another turn. Whatever the muse of history would write, a new assertiveness had come to the fore. Evidence of Black consciousness, of racial pride, was pervasive. Blacks were searching for new concepts and ideas or reviving old ones— Nationalism, Pan-Africanism, Marxism, Separatism, etc. The quickening pace of African liberation, which brought into the halls of independence one African country after another, was led by Kwame Nkrumah with the independence of Ghana in 1957, two years after Dr. King set the Civil Rights Movement in motion in Montgomery, Alabama. Events were moving frighteningly fast, and new leaders were catapulted to the world stage.

Alas, for the majority of Christians, Black and white, including theologians and Bible scholars, the new thrust—or resurfacing of the old (it had been done before)—did not win their allegiance. This was unfortunate because the Black church could have continued to exert great influence on the movement. If only it had recognized its own ideals, it could have staked its claim to the new development and provided inspiration and direction to the new thrust, perhaps keeping its children within the faith. Things might have been different. "Of all the words of tongue or pen, the saddest are these: It might have been."

For those still struggling with the faith, these were tough times. Anyone striving to theologize the developments, or to suggest that God wanted His people to understand and become involved, was repudiated by his fellow believers and dismissed by the nonbelievers. This was particularly true within fundamentalist circles. I personally spent several years trying to make evangelicals, white and Black, understand (not accept, mind you, but just *understand*) what was happening . It was a frustrating task that I eventually concluded was hopeless.

There were some who were trying to hear what God was saying and discern His presence. James Cone, Preston Williams, Albert Cleague, Gayraud Wilmore and Cornell West in the U.S.A.; Reuben Alves and Gustavo Gutierrez in South America; M. M. Thomas in India; and Burgess Carr and John S. Mbiti in Africa were some of those who were wrestling with the question of what we ought to be doing and saying with reference to God's will.

For the activists, radicals, or revolutionaries, however, particularly those with fundamental Biblical faiths, these were lonely times, a veritable no-man's land. We were saddled with the perception of Jesus as a pale-faced European, who always sided with our enemies and who urged us to be passive and nonviolent even under the most oppressive of conditions.

But was the portrayal and the perception of that portrayal true? Who really was this Jesus of history? What was His origin? What were His features? And what did He do in His environment? Was He always nonviolent, passive, going the extra mile, giving the other cheek, or was He urging the most viable option available?

How did He behave toward the oppressed? The poor? The sick? The hungry? How did He relate to oppressors? The structures of exploitation? Did He ignore them? If not, what did He do? Was He an activist? A radical? Was He perhaps a revolutionary?

Notes

1. Charles M. Sheldon, *In His Steps* (New York: Holt, Rhinehart, and Winston, 1935).
2. George G. M. James, *Stolen Legacy* (self-published, 1954, reprinted Trenton: Africa World Press, 1992)
3. Malcolm X, *On Afro American History* (New York: Path Finder Press, 1967), p. 64.
4. Walter Rodney, *How Europe Under-Developed Africa* (Washington: Howard University Press, 1974).
5. John Hope Franklin, *From Slavery to Freedom* (New York: Alfred A. Knopf, 1980).
6. Ibid., pp. 32-33.
7. J.C. DeGraft-Johnson, *African Glory* (New York: Walker and Company, 1965), P. 50.
8. Ibid.

PART II

THE ORIGIN OF JESUS

A good place to commence this search is in the Old Testament, and
—strangely enough—not among the usual messianic predictions,
shadows, and symbolism, but rather in the pedigree of Noah. In
Genesis 9:20-26, we read:

> And Noah began to be an husbandman, and he planted a
> vineyard: And he drank of the wine, and was drunken; and
> he was uncovered within his tent. And Ham, the father of
> Canaan, saw the nakedness of his father, and told his two
> brethren without. And Shem and Japtheth took a garment,
> and laid it upon both their shoulders and bend backward,
> and covered the nakedness of their father; and their faces
> were backward, and they saw not their father's nakedness.
> And Noah awoke from his wine, and knew what his younger
> son had done unto him. And he said, Cursed be Canaan; a
> servant of servants shall he be unto his brethren. And he
> said, Blessed be the Lord God of Shem; and Canaan shall
> be his servant.

This is one of the passages that oppressors have employed to justify their exploitation of Black humanity. Since Ham means "blackness," Noah, they said, cursed Ham and therefore all Black people
are cursed to be the servants of white people. However, when we
study the story carefully, we see that (if the curse means anything
at all) Noah cursed not Ham but Canaan.

Moreover, Ham had *other* sons who where builders of civilizations. For our purposes, we will focus on just two of them, Cush
and Mizraim.

> And the sons of Ham; Cush, and Mizraim, and Phut, and Canaan. And the sons of Cush; Seba, and Havilah, and Sabtah, and Raamah, and Sabtechah; and the sons of Raamah; Sheba and Dedan. And Cush begat Nimrod; he began to be a mighty one in the earth. (Genesis 10:6-8)

Shinar—Mesopotamia—Sumer

Cush, Ham's firstborn, can also be translated *Ethiopia*, which means "black or burnt-faced," and which was located in the area that has been called at various times Mesopotamia, Shinar, and what is today Iraq. In this general region were the Babylonians and Assyrians, but deeper than these, or before them, was the ancient civilization of Sumer, which goes back 6000 to 7000 years. It was a civilization of extraordinary achievements. According to the Bible, the children of Cush (blackness) inherited the region.

One of Cush's most famous sons was Nimrod, who, according to the Bible, was a great hunter or builder. Nimrod is given credit for building Babylon. Significantly, he has been identified with Hammurabi, famous for, among other things, the Code of Hammurabi. We should remember that it is from this region that Abraham came.

Also of interest is the fact that some Bible scholars believe the Garden of Eden can be located in this area. When we observe the rivers that surround the Garden, two have been identified as the Tigris and Euphrates and the other called Gihon is said to encompass the whole land of Ethiopia (Genesis 2:10-14). If Ethiopia is where we have always located it—in East Africa—how can a river flow from it to Eden, which is in Asia? The answer can only be in the blackness of the entire region.

The authors of the Bible saw blackness—Ethiopia—as the beginning of civilization. This included parts of Asia and Africa. The Garden of Eden, then, was in the land of blackness. This is consistent with secular research. The geographical area under discussion has been identified with blackness by Chancellor Williams: On the flyleaf of *The Destruction of Black Civilization* (1976), we read:

> "What became of the Black people of Sumer?" The traveler asked the old man, "for ancient records show that the people

of Sumer were black. What happened to them?" "Ah," the old man sighed, "They lost their history, so they died...."[1]

Also, Charles Silberman admitted that the Bible writers viewed this area as African.

> The Biblical language itself thus shows clearly that the ancients viewed Egypt as a Black society. Lest there be any doubt of the role of the Black men in that period, the author of Genesis continues by listing the sons of Ham. The oldest was Cush, the Biblical name for Ethiopia and down to the present, the vernacular Hebrew term for a black African. (Genesis reports that in addition to a number of other children, Cush "begot Nimrod, who was the first man of power of earth. He was a mighty hunter by the grace of the Lord," not to mention his having been the founder of Babylonia. The Israelites clearly believed that the Babylonians and Assyrians were of African origin — a belief shared by some contemporary historians.) The other children of Ham included Mizraim, the most common Biblical name for Egypt; Phut, or Libya; and Canaan, a name derived from a root meaning "to be low;" and referring originally to the low-lying coast of Phoenicia and the lowlands of the Philistines, later to all of western Palestine.[2]

Ethiopia—Land of the Beginnings

It is indisputable that blackness, or Ethiopia, held a high place in the ancient world. W.E.B. DuBois stated:

> In Ethiopia the sunrise of human culture took place spreading down into the Nile Valley. Ethiopia, land of the blacks, was thus the cradle of Egyptian civilization.
>
> Beyond Ethiopia, in Central and South Africa, lay the gold of Ophir and the rich trade of Punt on which the prosperity of Egypt largely depended. Egypt brought slaves from black Africa as she did from Europe and Asia. But, she also brought citizens and leaders from black Africa.
>
> When Egypt conquered Asia, she used black soldiers to a wide extent. When Asia overwhelmed Egypt, Egypt sought refuge in Ethiopia, as a child returns to its mother, and Ethiopia then for centuries dominated Egypt and successfully invaded Asia.

Neither Greece, Rome, nor Islam succeeded in conquering Ethiopia, although they pushed her pack and shut her up in East and Central Africa, hindered at all contact between her people and the world until the day of colonial imperialism.[3]

Silberman, who admits that there is some evidence that the Mesopotamians were black, quotes Dioderus Siculus, a first-century Greek historian:

The Ethiopians conceived themselves to be of greater antiquity than any other nation; and it is probably that, born under the sun's path, its warmth may have ripened them earlier than other men. They supposed themselves to be the inventors of worship of festivals, of solemn assemblies, of sacrifices and every religious practice.[4]

We should keep in mind the Ethiopian claim, "inventors of worship, solemn assemblies, of sacrifice and every religious practice," for much of what has been associated with Judaism is found at a much earlier date in Ethiopia.

Mizraim—Egypt—Ethiopia's Daughter

Let us now turn to Ham's other son, Mizraim, which means "Egypt." No one argues against the accomplishments of Egyptian civilization. The only argument heard in a few quarters is whether or not the early Egyptians were black. Those who hold out for whiteness or anything but blackness manifest the same mentality that refuses to yield its illusion of divine sanction in the exploitation of other people's resources. To everyone but the most incorrigible Europocentric the facts are incontrovertible.

The ancient Egyptians were Negroes. The moral fruit of their civilization is to be counted among the assets of the black world. Instead of presenting itself to history as an insolvent debtor, that black world is the very initiator of the Western civilization flaunted before our eyes today. Pythagorean mathematics, the theory of the four elements of Thales of Miletus, Epicurean materialism, Platonic idealism, Judaism, Islam and modern science are rooted in Egyptian cosmogony and science. One needs only to mediate on Osiris, the redeemer-god, who sacrifices himself, dies and is resurrected to save mankind, a figure essentially identifiable with Christ.[5]

Significantly, though, according to Diop, Ethiopians considered Egypt to be one of their colonies.[6]

In any event, the Bible writers understood Egypt to be black. After all, Mizraim was the second son of Ham. It is important to establish the blackness of Egyptians because the Israelites spent over four hundred years in this country.

According to the Bible, Joseph's brothers sold him to the Midianites, who in turn brought him to Egypt. After many ordeals, Joseph became prime minister, a reward for interpreting the pharaoh's dream and advising him to prepare immediately, during the years of plenty for the years of leanness that would follow. The gracious pharaoh also told Joseph to bring his family to Egypt, and he gave them the land of Goshen. There were 70 souls; Jacob, the old patriarch brought with him to Egypt just 70 starving cultureless nomads.[7]

When they departed hundreds of years later, the Bible said they took silver and gold. "Israel also came into Egypt; and Joseph sojourned in the land of Ham" (Psalm 105:23).

But they took more than silver and gold. They also carried with them Egyptian or African culture, art, philosophy, and religion. Even circumcision and sacrifice, according to Herodotus, were ancient practices of the Egyptians.[8] Monotheism occurred in Egypt a long time before Jacob entered that land. The scripture writers, identifying Cush as Ham's first-born, agreed with the Ethiopians' own estimate of themselves.

In a word, the few souls who came into Egypt were swallowed up or assimilated the culture of the Egyptians. When they departed they were really more African than anything else because Egyptians were African. How could it be otherwise? A small, insecure group coming into a country of teeming masses would surely have been assimilated into the dominant culture.

The time continuum in the history of the blacks is highly important in reference to the state of civilization in the lands from which the invading groups came during the first thousand years of black ascendency in Egypt, and southern incursive groups were largely tent-dwelling nomads. They had no tradition of great cities with imposing temples, obelisks, pyramids or indeed, stone masonry at all. In particular, one should note the number of centuries after

Thebes and Memphis before their ancient cities were founded:

Nowe (Thebes) Prehistory
Memphis 3100 B.C.
Babylon 2100 B.C.
Jerusalem 1400 B.C.
Athens (Village) 1200 B.C.
Rome (Village) 1000 B.C.
Antioch 400 B.C.
Athens (City) 360 B.C.
Rome (Town) 250 B.C.

In short, what great contributions did these roaming nomads have to make to an already highly developed black civilization? Since even Jerusalem was not in existence, what people in Lower Egypt came from a country with a city as great as Thebes or Memphis?[9]

We need look no further than Black people in the U.S.A. Our origin is African. But after four hundred years, we are more American than anything else. Whether we like it or not, we have been assimilated. This has happened to Blacks even when millions were involved. Imagine only 70 Blacks dwelling among millions of Europeans for 400 years.

We cannot overemphasize the point. When God liberated the Israelites, the hundreds of thousands of people who came forth were not the 70 people who went in. They were now Africans. If their stay in Egypt were not enough to Africanize them, their sojourn in Canaan, another black land, would have done it. Canaan, meaning "low-lying," you remember, was the grandson of Noah, he was the cursed child.[10]

Rudolph Windsor quotes the Talmud, which claims that Africans came to Alexander the Great, asking him for the land of Canaan, thus validating the Africanness of Canaan.[11]

Throughout their stay in Canaan's land, there was widespread miscegenation; and to further mix things up, in 721, the Assyrians conquered Israel and carried away all but one tribe—Judah (II Chronicles 36:1-21). Then, in 605 B.C., the Babylonians duplicated the feat of the Assyrians and carried most of the people to Babylon, at least those who did not escape into Egypt (II Kings 17:13-31; Jeremiah 52:28-30).[12] While in Babylon, most of the Israelites became well integrated into the society. There was more mixing with the Persians, who conquered the Babylonians; and then mixing with the Greeks, Syrians, Romans, and God only knows who else. So by the time Jesus came, He could accurately say that He was the "Son of Man."[13] The people who by now were called Jews were the compilation of many cultures, of many lands; and while color would have to be de-emphasized, it is still worth noting that the description of Jesus in the Book of Revelation, indicated that He had still retained some of these African features.

> His head and his hairs were white like wool, as white as snow; and his eyes were as a flame of fire; And his feet like unto fine brass, as if they burned in a furnace; and his voice as the sound of many waters. (Revelations 1:14-15).

The Curse of Ham—Its Origin and Distortion
Since we have seen that to the Scripture writers, the early civilizations were Black in origin, how then did the story of Noah cursing Ham come about and from that allocate all black people as servants of white people? Let me quote two sources:

Here we have reached the historical background of the curse upon Ham. It is not by chance that this curse on the father of Mizraim, Phut, Cush and Canaan, fell only on Canaan, who dwelt in a land that the Jews have coveted throughout their history.

Whence came this name Ham (Cham, Kam)? Where could Moses have found it? Right in Egypt where Moses was born, grew up, and lived until the Exodus. In fact, we know that the Egyptians called their country *Kemit*, which means "black" in their language. The interpretation according to which Kemit designates the black soil of the country of the blacks stems from a gratuitous distortion by minds aware of what an exact interpretation of this would imply.

Hence, it is natural to find Kam in Hebrew, meaning "heat," "black," or "burned." That being so, all apparent contradictions disappear, and the logic of facts appears in all its nudity. The inhabitants of Egypt, symbolized by their black color, Kemit or Ham of the Bible, would be accursed in the literature of the people they had oppressed. We can see that this biblical curse on Ham's offspring had an origin quite different from that generally given it today without the slightest historical foundation. What we cannot understand, however, is how it has been possible to make a white race of Kemit;

Hamite, black ebony, etc. (even in Egyptian). Obviously, according to the needs of the cause, Ham is cursed, blacked, and made into the ancestor of the Negroes. This is what happens whenever one refers to contemporary social relations.

On the other hand, he is whitened whenever one seeks the origin of civilization, because there he is inhabiting the first civilized country in the world. So the idea of Eastern and Western Hamites is conceived—"nothing more than a convenient invention to deprive blacks of the moral advantage of Egyptian civilization and of other African civilizations, as we shall see..."[14]

The erroneous belief that Ham was cursed stems in part from the ambiguity of the verses immediately preceding the curse, in part from mistranslation. They are usually translated: "Ham, the father of Canaan, saw his father's nakedness and told his two brothers outside. And Noah awoke from his wine and knew what *his youngest son* had done unto him." [Emphasis added.] The first verse does suggest that the sin (of looking at Noah's nakedness) was committed by Ham—but the text curiously identifies Ham as "the father of Canaan."

The fact that it was Canaan and not Ham who was guilty seems clear from study of the next few verses. For one thing, the curse is clearly directed at Canaan, not at Ham. For another, the line preceding the curse is invariably translated incorrectly. It should read, "and Noah knew what his grandson had done unto him." The Hebrew word *beno hakatan* may either be translated "his youngest son" or "his grandson" (the latter meaning is similar to the French petit-fils.) But "grandson" is the correct, indeed the only possible translation in this instance, for Ham was not Noah's youngest son, Japheth was the youngest; Ham was the middle son. (See Genesis VI, 1; VII, 13; IV, 18; X,1.)[15]

First of all, what we see, according to Silberman, is that the curse was never directed toward Ham, but Canaan. Then Diop raises another possibility. The curse was placed upon Canaan or "blackness" because the authors of the Bible were servants of Mizraim, "blackness," in Egypt. And second, the land of Canaan was coveted by the Israelites. Just as the American Indians were savages or cursed in the view of whites who wanted their land, so a similar situation took place with the sons of Ham in ancient times.

Whether or not we agree with Diop's explanation of the curse is not the most important thing. Rather it is important that we agree that the sons of Ham were not cursed, but were the builders of civilization.

In *African Origins of the Major "Western Religions,"*[16] Dr. Josef ben-Jochannan argues that European religion is rooted in Africa, and therefore, Jesus would have an African origin. Dr. Ben and others believe that in the stories of Osiris is the origin of the death and resurrection story of Jesus. As with Diop, so with "Doctor Ben," it is not necessary to accept all their explanations and theories. What is of paramount importance is that they all agree on the African beginning of all things, including religion, and that includes Jesus Christ.

For blacks, trying to break the chains of a Europeanization of Jesus, to be able to declare on firm historical grounds, secular and biblical, that Jesus has a black past, an African origin, is profoundly significant.

Notes

1. Chancellor Williams, *The Destruction of Black Civilization* (Chicago: Third World Press, 1976).
2. Charles E. Silberman, *Crisis in Black and White* (New York: Vintage Books, 1976), p. 173.

    Even Will Durant paid tribute to the region under discussion by admitting that practically everything of value comes from his area of the globe: "Sumerian civilization may be summed up in this contrast between crude pottery and consummate jewelry; it was synthesis of rough beginnings and occasional but brilliant mastery. Here, within the limits of our present knowledge, are the first states and empires, the first irrigation, the first use of gold and silver as standards of value, the first business contracts, the first credit system, the first code of law, the first extensive development of writing, the first stories of the Creation and the Flood, the first sculpture and bas-relief, the first palaces and temples, the first ornamental mental and decorative themes, the first arch, column, vault, and dome. Here, for the first known time on a large scale, appear some of the sins of civilization: slavery despotism, ecclesiasticism, and imperialistic war.... It was a life differentiated and subtle, abundant and complex. Already the natural inequality of men was producing a new degree of comfort and luxury for the strong, and a new routine of hard and disciplined labor for the rest. The theme was struck on which history would strum its myriad variations." See Will Durant, *Story of Civilization*, Part I, (New York: Simon and Schuster, 1954), p. 134.

He even admits that the "Aryans" took civilization from the Babylonians and Egyptians: "The Aryans did not establish civilization—they took it from Babylonia and Egypt. Greece did not begin civilization—it inherited far more civilization than it began; it was the spoiled heir of three millenniums of arts and sciences brought to its cities from the Near East by the fortunes of trade and ware. In studying and honoring the Near East we shall be acknowledging a debt long due to the real founders of European and American civilization" (Ibid., p. 116.)

Durant fails to acknowledge the blackness or Africaness of the area. But other scholars do and, again to emphasize, the Bible acknowledges that Blackness was the origin.

3. W.E.B. Dubois, *The World and Africa* (New York: International Publishers, 1965), p. 117.

4. Ibid., p. 172.

5. Cheikh Anta Diop, *The African Origin of Civilization* (New York: Lawrence Hill & Company, 1974), p. xiv.

6. Ibid., p. 1.

7. For the story of Joseph's enslavement and the 400-year story of the Israelites in Egypt, see Genesis 37-48.

8. All Egyptians used bulls and bull calves for sacrifice, if they have passed the test for cleanness; but they were forbidden to sacrifice cows, for cows were sacred to Isis. See Herodotus, *The Histories* (New York: Penguin Books, 1954), p. 145.

My own idea on the subject was based first on the fact that (they) Colchians have black skins and wooly hair (not that that amounts to much, as other nations have the same), and secondly, and more especially, on the fact that the Colchians, the Egyptians, and the Ethiopians are the only races from ancient times to have practiced circumcision. The Phoenicians and the Syrians of Palestine themselves admit that they adopted the practice from Egypt, and the Syrians who lived near the rivers Thermodon and Parthenius, as well as their neighbors the Macronians, say that they learnt if only a short time ago from the Colchians. No other nations use circumcision, and all these are without doubt following the Egyptian lead (Ibid., p. 167).

9. Williams, p. 69.

10. See *"Was Jesus Black?"* a tract by Rev. Herbert Daughtry, the House

of the Lord Church, 415 Atlantic Ave., Brooklyn, NY 11217.

11. Rudolph R. Windsor, *From Babylon to Timbuktu* (New York: Exposition Press, 1969), p. 106.

12. The first use of the word "Jew" in the Bibile with reference to the Israelites is by the prophet Jeremiah. It should also be noted that it is Africans and Asians who dominate. Europe's role is insignificant. It is basically the Near East or the fertile crescent where all the action takes place. And again Africans and black Asians, the sons of Ham, are the centers of influence.

13. Windsor, p. 35. Windsor, in the summary of Chapter IV, demonstrates the blackness of the Israelites: "There is more than enough evidence to prove that all the original Israelites were black, including the surrounding nations in the Middle East; we must consider the evidence that the Dravidians were the original Black people of India; that the Cushites (Ethiopians) inhabited the southern Mesopotamian Valley; that Abraham and Ishmael married African women (Egyptians); that the Canaanites belong to the African family of nations; that ancient Israel intermarried with these black Canaanite tribes; at the time that Joseph was viceroy of Egypt his brothers could not distinguish him from the black Egyptians because Joseph was black; after Pharaoh promulgated the cruel decree to extirpate the Hebrew males, only a black Moses would have been able to be concealed effectively for any length of time among black Egyptians; that Daniel had a dream of an anthropomorphous God with wooly hair; that biblical leprosy laws of the time could apply only to a very dark people with black hair. The black Jews of India, Abyssinia (Ethiopia), and West Africa consider themselves the original Jews because of the purity of their Israelite blood; this has been stated by Allen H. Godbey."

14. Diop, pp. 7, 9.

15. Silberman, p. 174.

16. Josef ben-Jochannan, *African Origins of the Major "Western Religions"* (New York: Alkebu-Lan Books, 1970).

PART III

SEARCH FOR A REVOLUTIONARY JESUS FOR A REVOLUTIONARY AGE

While there is satisfactory evidence that Jesus was African in origin, there was and is still the problem of his alleged passivity. Even a Black "turn the other cheek" Jesus would not solve the problem. So again, the question is, Was Jesus always passive, mild speaking, nonviolent, and what would He do today in the U.S.A. if He were black? When we study the words and actions of Jesus in the context of His society and in the framework of our knowledge, as limited as that is, there is enough evidence to suggest that Jesus' passivity is more imagined than real.

It is important that we remember that much of Jesus' ministry was conducted under the scrutiny of His enemies, who were always trying to trap Him. This obviously necessitated a coded means of communication. Thus, the same words used by the adversary, when used by Jesus could have a different meaning, depending on the emphasis, the facial expression, and the body movement.

Revolutionary Rhetoric

Consider some of these statements and actions. At the synagogue in Nazareth, Jesus read from the prophets:

> And he came to Nazareth, where he had been brought up: and, as his custom was, he went into the synagogue on the sabbath day, and stood up for to read. And there was delivered unto him the book of the prophet Esaias. And when he had opened the book he found the place where it is written, The Spirit of the Lord is upon me, because he

> hath anointed me to preach the gospel to the poor; he hath
> sent me to heal the brokenhearted, to preach deliverance to
> the captives, and recovering of sight to the blind, to set at
> liberty them that are bruised; To preach the acceptable year
> of the Lord. (Luke 4:16-19)

In addition to his expression of concern for the physical well-being of human beings, there were a couple of phrases that could have double meanings. "Open the prison doors and setting the captives free"—was He referring to prison as we think of prison, or was He referring to spiritual prisons or some kind of oppression? Then He said, "to proclaim the acceptable year of the Lord." Was He calling for the cancellation of all debts? If so, wasn't that a revolutionary call? If today someone urged nonpayment of debts, including taxes, how would it be viewed by the government?

Similarly, note the rather ambiguous response of Jesus to a loaded question: Should taxes be paid to Caesar? "Render unto Caesar the things that are Caesar's, unto God the things that are God's" (Matthew: 22:21). Was that as innocuous as it appeared, or was that a coded message? Was Jesus really saying what Judas of Galilee had said, i.e., Don't pay? Judas of Galilee had led a tax revolt some years earlier, declaring that everything in Palestine belonged to God (Acts 5:37).

And what about those scathing attacks upon the illustrious leaders who embodied law and tradition; and His condemnation of the system? "You have made it a den of thieves" (Matthew 21:1-11) are heavy words.

Just the words alone without accompanying denunciation of revolutionaries and radicals would evoke question regarding the intention of the utterer. But when actions are added . . . .

Action

The entry of Jesus into Jerusalem was in fulfillment of Zechariah's prophesy. His ride into Jerusalem on what we call Palm Sunday (Luke 9:51-54) raises questions regarding His motives. Jesus was the son of David, the warrior King whose kingdom God promised to establish. Surely, then, Jesus knew the crowd that greeted Him on this festive occasion, understood the military significance of this entry. "Hosanna," they shouted, "Blessed is he who comes in the name of the Lord. Blessed be the Kingdom of our Father who is coming" (Matthew 20:20-23).

Certainly there wasn't anything peaceful about His action in the temple when He attacked the licensed businessmen, uttering the words already quoted (Matthew 26:50-52). Would any leader bent on peace attack the economic system and its respected merchants, especially when they were wrapped in religious garb? Did Jesus know He was casting down the gauntlet? Does His action in the temple area on behalf of exploited poor folks prove that Jesus was a leader who was willing to risk all in an assault on the system on behalf of others?

Jesus' Friends and Disciples

Next, look at the people who were attracted to Him—the common people, the winos, prostitutes, the outcasts, tax swindlers, zealots, revolutionaries. Is that kind of catering to and organizing of the outcast, misfits, radicals, and revolutionaries the efforts of a leader with no concern for structural change?

Among his inner circle there were some characters with rather shady backgrounds. Had they all been converted to an individual, other-worldly salvation living in peace and goodwill with Romans and their own countrymen? Or did they believe that Jesus was the Messiah who would restore the kingdom of Israel—a real, earthly, material, concrete kingdom? And if this was their thinking, did Jesus know it? Did he lead them on, or was he planning to fulfill their expectations?

Consider Judas Iscariot. *Iscariot* bears a striking resemblance to *Sicarii*, the word used by Josephus to identify the knife wielders, the dagger men who had developed a skill of killing people with daggers hidden in their sleeves.

It has been suggested that the only plausible reason for Judas' betrayal of Jesus was that Jesus was not militant enough. Jesus really intended to be peaceful. But if he, Judas, could force Jesus to act, Jesus surely would enjoin the battle and issue a call for the masses to join Him. Judas was a Zealot, and Zealots did not sell out to Romans for a few pieces of silver. On the contrary, they would die themselves, for nothing, if it meant promoting their cause.

Then there was Simon the Zealot, and James and John, the two firebrand brothers, called by Jesus the "sons of thunder." The term

Boanerges from which "thunder" is translated, can also be translated "the fierce and wrathful ones." James and John, true to their nature, wanted to rain fire from heaven on a Samaritan village that denied passageway to Jesus (Luke 9:52-54). If they would burn up a people for so minimal act, what would they do to murderous Romans and treacherous Israelites. And these same brothers were ambitious too. They wanted the right and left hand on the throne.[1] Additionally, the disciples carried swords too. On the night the authorities came for Jesus, Peter went for his piece and adroitly wacked the ear off the head of one of the policemen (Matthew 24:29-45). Granted, Jesus reattached the ear, but why did He allow Peter to pack the sword in the first place? Surely he knew Peter was packing. You cannot hide a sword as one might hide a switchblade. Did all of them carry swords? If so, what for? What would "turn the other cheek" disciples following a "go the extra mile" leader want with swords?

Ghettos of Nazareth
The place of Jesus' child-rearing, Nazareth, was a hell hole, a ghetto. No good thing ever came from Nazareth, went the proverb. Nazareth was a hotbed of revolutionary activity. There had been a Zealot uprising around 6 A.D. Jesus grew up in the knowledge of the heroics of the Zealots. Can a leader with that kind of background be inflexibly wedded to peaceful tactics? In the early years of His community there were attempts to eradicate class lines and to have everyone shared equitably. Was this socialism? Also, there was the removal of discrimination based on sex. Everyone was equal in Jesus' community (Acts 2:44,45). Was this a statement? Did Jesus know that to teach and to build an alternative community, where everyone was equal and shared all things equally, would automatically condemn social orders predicated upon class structures?

Tradition of the Prophets
And what about the tradition of the prophets, the tradition Jesus followed? They were known to lead armies, fight guerilla warfare, and do whatever was necessary to promote God's will, as they understood it.[2]

Eschatological Statement

And finally, Jesus' eschatological statement, with its blood and war dramatics (Matthew 24:29-45). Was it meant only for the future?

In other words, was Jesus a revolutionary only in individual conversion and future expectation? No one can deny that in each of the above two areas Jesus was a revolutionary. But can revolution be dichotomized? Can there be a revolutionary individual without that individual living out that revolution in impactful ways within society?

Carl Braaten writes in *The Future of God—The Revolutionary Dynamics of Hope*:

> The simple fact of preaching the gospel is like putting sticks of dynamite into the social structure.[3]

Similarly, does a glimpse of a new order, even in the future, inspire efforts to change the present to conform to that future? Braaten, in *Christ and Counter-Christ,* wrote:

> The power of Jesus' freedom is eschatological, but the place of its realization is history.[4]

Is this the kind of revolution Jesus finally settled for after months of agonizing on tactics, programs, strategies, allies, and goals? To admit that still makes Jesus a revolutionary, and also, if the above is true, does that not place upon Him responsibility for His people's actions, even when that action is violent confrontation with demonic structures? Jesus surely knew what Frederick Douglass, 1800 years after him, knew: "Power concedes nothing without a demand." One who radically alters a person's self-concept and worldview so that that person now works for the liberation of others thus bringing that person into conflict with the status quo, must bear some of the legal and moral responsibility for that person's behavior.

Apparently Contradictory Statements by Jesus

> Blessed are the peacemakers. (Matthew 5:9)

> Think not that I am come to send peace on earth: I came not to send peace, but a sword. (Matthew 10:34)

> Whosoever shall smite thee on thy right cheek, turn to him the other also. (Matthew 5:39)

> Suppose ye that I am come to give peace on earth? I tell you, Nay; but rather division. (Luke 12:51)

> All they that take the sword shall perish with the sword. (Matthew 26:52)

> He that hath no sword, let him sell his garment, and buy one. (Luke 22:36)

> Love your enemies, do good to them which hate you. (Luke 6:27)

> And when he had made a scourge of small cords, he drove them all out of the temple... and poured out the changers' money, and overthrew the tables. (John 2:15)

What is the reason for these apparently contradictory scriptures? Marvin Harris in his book, *Cows, Pigs, Wars and Witches: The Riddle of Culture*, put forth the claim that the idea of a peaceful messiah came to fruition after the destruction of Jerusalem in 71 A.D.

From the stress Mark placed upon the destruction of the temple in Jerusalem as a punishment for the killers of Jesus, Brandon infers that this gospel—the first to be composed and the model for the others—was written in Rome after the fall of Jerusalem. As Brandon says, it was probably written in direct response to the great victory celebration of 71 A.D.

The appropriate conditions for the spread of the cult for a peaceful messiah were at last present in full force. Jewish Christians now readily joined with gentile converts to convince the Romans that their messiah was different from the Zealot-branded messiahs who had caused the war, and who were continuing to make trouble: Christians, unlike Jews, were harmless pacifists with no secular ambitions. The Christian Kingdom of God was not of this world; Christian salvation lay in eternal life beyond the grave; the Christian messiah had died to bring eternal life to all mankind; his teaching posed no threat to the Romans, only to the Jews; the Romans were absolved of any guilt in Jesus' death; the Jews alone had killed him while Pontius Pilate stood by, helplessly unable to prevent it.[5]

Christians Are Led by The Spirit

Enough questions have been posed to demonstrate that it is not a simple matter to know what Jesus would do at any given time and place, and that to make passivity an inflexible tactic based upon Jesus as revealed in scripture is a shaky proposition.

What all this says is that people of God are moved by the Spirit to act in the highest manner possible. There are no fixed maps to be given ahead of time. But is this not faith; to believe that God will guide in every situation? To say what one will or will not do is not necessarily faith. But to say one will do whatever is the right thing to do, for God will not allow it otherwise, is a declaration of faith.

This is not to suggest that there is no ideal. God's people—of all people—have ideals. They have seen the Lord. They have a foretaste of glory. But ideals cannot always be realized.

Oftentimes, maybe most times, we are forced to choose between what is bad and what is worse. How do we know what to choose? God will guide us, faith affirms.

Why the Question—What Would Jesus Do?

Why this search for a Jesus that is relevant in a revolutionary situation? The obvious reason is we want to do the will of the Lord. For ourselves, yes, but also for others. If we knew what Jesus would do, who knows what a difference that could make. Carl Braaten lists three reasons we need to be involved:

> In order to practice Christian hope for the world, we must reflect on whether or how God may be active in revolutionary situations. There is a very practical reason why we as Christians need a theology of revolution. Without it we will be at a total loss about what to do for the rest of the century.

Then he quotes Hannah Arendt in her book on revolution:

In the contest which divides the world today and in which
so much is at stake, those will probably win who understand revolution.

Another reason he cites is:

The church is, to a large extent, responsible for the revolutionary consciousness that is emerging around the world.
Indirectly the church has sponsored the revolutionary process by preaching a message which sets things in motion
by stirring up the imagination, arousing new expectations,
and stimulating a crusading zeal to translate hopes, whose
realization some would postpone for heaven above, already
into the social structures of this world.

Another reason is the imperative for repentance on the part of the
church. They stimulated or created the revolutionary process and
then attempted to stifle it or walk away from it. Braaten states:

While the gospel they preached pointed the way of hope
for the future, the institutions they built impeded its coming. The official churches—as well as church officials—
have been guilty of betraying the promises of the gospel
for the sake of securing alliances with the classes tenured
with privileges of power, property and position.[6]

Martin E. Marty, in his book *The Search for a Usable Future*,
agrees with Braaten but warns that:

One would hope that the churches would take part not in
order to attract attention, [not] to be relevant, [not] to assert their virility, but because of human need expressed in
the situation. Nor need Christians step out of their role and
stop being the church. They do not exist in order to become a revolutionary (or anti-revolutionary) political party
but to do what situations demand, and situations demand
more things and other things than being revolutionaries.
Christians cannot, however, fulfill their missions and man-
dates without coming to some sort of terms with that aspect of life covered by the term revolution or radical social

change. The alternative is to put oneself as a priority on the side of the status quo, no matter how evil and dehumanizing it be.[7]

The Particular Role of Black Christians

There is another reason for Black Christians. The places where the revolutions are taking place, for the most part, are Third World countries. The battle is on to win back land and resources. Black Christians are in a crucial position. They can play a critical role in the movements, or they can opt to side with the opposition. They cannot be neutral. To do nothing in the face of an evil is in some sense to perpetuate that evil.

Mention has already been made of an opportunity lost during the latter stages of the Civil Rights Movement, because God's people could not recognize their own language and ideas, and because they thought of Jesus in European limitation.

Harvey Cox mentioned a similar situation concerning Cuba, as quoted in Vernon C. Grounds' book entitled *Revolution and the Christian Faith*:

> It is reported that during the initial stages of Castro's movement, before he came into power and even for a short time thereafter, there were a number of Cuban Baptists in high positions in his movement. But, when they found a real revolution on their hands and wanted to make a Christian witness and contribution within a revolutionary situation, they were totally baffled. . . . These Cuban Christians lacked the kind of theology of the world that we have begun to develop; perhaps if they had not retreated the story in Cuba might have been different.[8]

Black followers of Jesus Christ have one more opportunity to bring their special dimension to this revolutionary age. They need to think hard and pray hard. This may be their moment in history. It may be that God has called them to this time to be the vanguard people—to proclaim salvation to the nations in the most comprehensive meaning of salvation.

Notes

1. Reverend Herbert Daughtry, "A Theology of Black Liberation from a Black Perspective: The What, Who and How," *The Virginia Seminary Journal*, XXVI (January 1974).

2. Ibid.

3. Carl E. Braaten, *The Future of God—The Revolutionary Dynamics of Hope* (New York: Harper & Row, 1969), p. 143.

4. Carl E. Braaten, *Christ and Counter-Christ* (Philadelphia: Fortress Press, 1972), p. 30.

5. Marvin Harris, *Cows, Pigs, Wars, and Witches, The Riddles of Culture* (New York: Vantage Books, 1975), pp. 201, 202.

6. Braaten, *The Future of God*, pp. 142, 143.

7. Martin E. Marty, *The Search for a Usable Future* (New York: Harper & Row, 1969), p. 107.

8. Vernon C. Grounds, *Revolution and the Christian Faith* (New York: J.B. Lippincott Co., 1971), p. 72.

PART IV

JESUS, THE SURPRISING CONTEMPORARY (A)— REDEEMING IN ACTION

There is a fountain filled with blood,
Drawn from Immanuel's veins,
And sinners plunged beneath that flood,
Lose all their guilty stains.

— Christian Hymn

For as much as ye know that ye were not redeemed with corruptible things, as silver and gold, from your vain conversation received by tradition from your fathers;

But with the precious blood of Christ, as of a lamb without blemish and without spot:

Who verily was foreordained before the foundation of the world, but was manifest in these last times for you.

— I Peter 1:18-20

In the next several weeks I want to invite you to think with me about Jesus the Christ. The title "Jesus, the Surprising Contemporary" is not original with me. I first heard it from a Dutch theologian in Thailand. He wanted to convey the idea that Jesus was startlingly relevant, that He confronts humanity in every age with His timeless message and person.

I thought at that time, what a striking characterization— Jesus, the Surprising Contemporary. It seemed to gather up in a dramatic and concise fashion my own thinking about Jesus. He is a contemporary, and He is relevant.

Whether we like it or not, if we engage in serious thinking, eventually we will meet Him, and He forces us to do something with Him. He seems always to be there.

Who was this Jesus called the Christ? Some called Him a friend of sinners and prostitutes; demon-possessed; an impostor; a blasphemer. Others called Him the Son of God, the Lamb of God, the Son of Man, a prophet, a Rabbi or teacher, the Messiah or Christ.

What did he call Himself? That always depended on with whom He was speaking. And when we read the Bible, we must always read it with an understanding that Jesus is always under surveillance. The establishment, the police, the spies are always present.

Sometimes they try to trap Him with questions. Other times they try to tangle up His words so that He is made to say what is not intended. They feel threatened by Him. He is gathering masses of people around Him. All kinds of people—the poor, Zealots or revolutionaries, the dispossessed. They are not sure what His aim is. Maybe He will start an insurrection, maybe a revolution. He must be stopped! So keep in mind that when Jesus speaks, or teaches, He knows enemies are around. He knows that eventually He will be killed, but He must take care that it does not happen before He has had time to build His movement.

So, what He calls Himself, and what He allows others to call Him, depends upon who is doing the calling and who is around at the time. I will discuss the names of Jesus and titles at another time — suffice it now to say that He accepted the title "Messiah" which is Hebrew; the Greek form is "Christ." The name means the "Anointed One."

It was believed that God would send a special representative to earth to save or to liberate mankind from its sinfulness in all of its manifestations and demonstrate His will to mankind.

The nation of Israel had been chosen by God to be the channel through which the Messiah would come, and all the people eagerly prayed and waited towards this end.

Now there are some problems posed by the so-called followers of Jesus, making it difficult for people to see His relevance. Sometimes the followers lock Him up in Heaven. They make Jesus some kind of "up-there spirit," totally removed from the tension and turmoil of ordinary, everyday earth living.

It was probably in reaction to this concept of Jesus that people began to talk about the search for the historical Jesus. They wanted to find the real flesh-and-blood Jesus. They wanted to be done with spirits and myths. They wanted the real historical Jesus.

One group locked Him up in heaven, and the other group locked Him in history. In neither instance, it would seem, did Jesus the surprising contemporary appear. In each case He was either up there, or back there, but not here and now.

Then, probably reacting to both of these, some theologians began talking about the Jesus who is "out there," ahead of us, beckoning us to come ahead. They talked about the future breaking in. In this view, the followers of Jesus are pilgrims; they have no stationary place; they must be continually pulling up stakes and moving on. For it is not the will of Jesus that His followers should become comfortable, or captured in any culture, condition, or state of being. They were to follow their Lord out into the future. This Dutch theologian also said, "I had to get rid of my Western baggage that I might follow Christ through culture." He meant that he had to cast aside worn-out value systems, outdated norms, old frames of reference, to follow Jesus, who was leading him into new life, styles and cultural expressions.

Now, I believe that Jesus as the surprising contemporary comprehends the best of those three approaches. It searches for and embraces the historical Jesus back there; it gathers to itself the spiritual Jesus located up there: and it merges the Jesus ahead of us, out there; thus, Jesus becomes contemporaneous with us— right here.

Now, what do I mean that Jesus is contemporary? The Pentecostal movement in America is an example of Jesus' relevance, or His contemporaneousness. The same Pentecostal movement is also an example of abortive development. *Pentecostal,* from a Greek word meaning "fiftieth," refers to a festive day which came fifty days after Passover in the calendar of the Israelites. It was the gathering of the first fruits, so there was great celebration. It was on this day that the disciples of Jesus were filled with the Holy Ghost, speaking in tongues. So, Pentecostalism has come to refer to those who believe in being filled with the spirit of God and evidencing that fact by speaking in tongues.

Now, the Pentecostal movement really got going in America around 1906, through the efforts of a black, one-eyed preacher named Charles Seymour. The place was an old Methodist Church, long since closed, in the city of Los Angeles, California. God demonstrated His presence miraculously, in healings of all kinds and in radically changed lives. But perhaps the greatest miracle was that color and class lines were broken down. Everybody was the same. There was a democratization of the gifts. People came from all over the world, and they carried the message back with them. Significantly, the Charismatic Movement that has since swept the world began in such humble surroundings.

Now, if this could have continued, if men and women would have permitted God to continue His work through them, we might have seen a change in American society. But in a few years, the Pentecostal Movement followed the racial and color pattens of the larger society. White men formed denominations and fellowships and groups with other white men and enjoyed the benefits of a racist institution. Instead of challenging, they conformed, and so the Spirit of Jesus was captured by culture.

Now, what is interesting, particularly for black Pentecostals and Evangelicals, is that they too, in another kind of way, became supporters of the status quo. They saw their roles as preaching against sin, and they defined sin in terms of short dresses, lipstick, movie shows, smoking, drinking, and pornography. Moreover, living holy came to mean not only refraining from the above, but also withdrawing from all protest and programs designed to confront the unjust institutions of America and waiting for Jesus to return from "up there" in heaven.

Instead of following Christ into new and perhaps radical expressions, our Pentecostal brothers turned away from it all, got holy, and frowned on others who were trying to change social conditions. Their worship became a kind of escapism. You went to church not to be informed, educated, enlightened, or challenged; you went there to have a "good time" ("in the Lord," of course); to "get high on God," as one preacher put it.

The only difference between white Pentecostalism and black Pentecostalism was color. Both were conservative; both supported the system either consciously (as was the case with most whites), or silently (as was the case with most blacks), for being silent in the face of injustice is to help sustain that injustice. As a result, many turned away from Jesus. But it wasn't really Jesus that they were rejecting. They were rejecting a *white* Jesus who was woven into an American racist, exploitative system, *not* the Jesus of Scripture—the surprising contemporary.

Jesus is relevant. He is here. He is real. We must seek Him as He is, and let Him express Himself, not according to our cultural patterns, but in whatever way He desires. It is then that we discover that He is in truth a startling contemporary. He meets us at the crossroads. He meets us in the market place, in the political arena, in the school room, in the barber shop, butcher shop, beauty shop. He meets us in the hospitals and in the institutions. He is the startling contemporary. He is inescapable. And when we meet Him, we will not be the same ever again.

When we seriously study the life of Jesus, as we shall have occasion to do in the weeks ahead, we shall be driven to the conclusion that Jesus was not a cheerful conformer to the systems of men, as his followers—through their own fears, ignorance, and self-interest—have often made Him out to be.

In every age, some would have Jesus adjusting to the contemporary cultures, value systems, mores, and styles of life. They would have Him accepting the prevailing political, religious, and social structures. But Jesus was not a this world conformer, waiting on another world. He was a confronter. He confronted men and women and societies with their sins, individually and collectively. Nobody was spared. The highest as well as the lowest came under His Judgement. But all were given the opportunity to start anew. He showed them that they could become the children of God.

He was a disturber of the peace. He disturbed the serene order of the *status quo*; the order built upon the gratification of the few and the degradation of the masses.

He was a shatterer. He shattered religious and social and political systems that were corrupt to the core.

In a word, He was a troublemaker. He just could not leave things alone. He always had to be meddling and poking around.

He came with a new order. And to inaugurate a new order it is always necessary to overturn or to remove the old order. Now that is true individually, and it is also true collectively. "You can't put new wine into old bottles," He once said, "nor can you put old wine into new bottles." New wine must be put in new bottles. You need a complete newness, newness through and through.

He came with a new ethic, a new morality, a new way of looking at old problems and questions. He came with a new value system, one not grounded in tribal preservation or ancient laws, but in the eternal rightness of things.

Now His disciples had learned their lesson well. For it was said of them that they were turning the world upside down. What a description: "These are they that have turned the world upside down." What did that description mean?

It meant that they rejected the world's idea of justice and rightness. It meant that they refused to accept society's concept of what was important and what was meaningful and what was authentic. It meant that the followers of Jesus, following the example of their Lord, went everywhere with a disdain for political, social, religious systems; they cared nothing for old moralities, old authorities, old traditions, etc. For these things had not brought peace and justice to the world, to say nothing of producing an abundancy for all earth's inhabitants. And, therefore, the disciples felt that these things needed to be swept aside to make way for the new order which would start in the minds and spirits of humanity and would issue forth into a new community comprised of all the people of the world, and give rise to new social structures.

Jesus had said, "My Kingdom is not of this world." What He meant was that His kingdom gathers its ethics, its rationale, its philosophy, its lifestyles, its values, its strategy, not from the systems of men, for these are bankrupt, for they are built upon the wisdom and self-interest of men. But rather, His kingdom is sustained and perpetuated by the infusion of the Eternal Spirit of the Almighty Himself, which captures the spirits of men and catapults them out into the world with messages of salvation for all; and, therefore, His Kingdom is incorruptible. Its treasures are in heaven, beyond the corruption of earth. You can't buy or bribe your way in; you've got to be born anew. You've got to undergo a radical reordering of your attitudes, values, associations, and desires.

His kingdom is irresistible, the gates of hell cannot stop it. And it is eternal, for it flows from God Himself. And it is always in opposition to the kingdom of this world, for the systems of men are demonic. They are conceived in pride, nurtured in arrogance, and raised on selfishness, yielding a harvest of injustice, violence, inhuman behavior, and misery. And one day His kingdom, though small and insignificant now, shall grow and grow and gather momentum with the passing years and shall destroy the systems of men, and a new nation will begin.

JESUS, THE SURPRISING CONTEMPORARY(B)

One of the most memorable experiences that I have ever had occurred in Bangkok, Thailand. We had concluded a three-year study on the theme "Salvation Today,"—sponsored by the Commission on World Mission and Evangelism. There were about fifteen of us present from various countries, including Japan, India, Korea, Geneva, Germany, and Africa. We gathered to discuss the theme "Giving Account for the Reason for the Hope Within Us." This was sponsored by the Faith and Order Commission of the World Council of Churches. I spent about five intensive day-and-night discussions with the group before I moved on to fulfill other commitments in Vietnam and Indonesia.

To repeat, it was an exhilarating, unforgettable experience. Our discussion covered many areas. We pondered the meaning of history and time as it is perceived from different cultures. We touched on the church worldwide, its strengths and weaknesses, and so on.

After several days, we discovered that our conversation invariably became "Christological," that is, Christ-centered. So, I think it is appropriate to our sermon topic for me to relate some of the thinking from at least four different countries. We would hope to see how Christ is a contemporary in different parts of the world. Also, and what I think is equally appropriate, we shall see conclusively that Christianity is not a white man's religion, decaying all over the world.

There is a big lie in the land, and its been around for some time now. It is that Christianity is the white man's religion, confined only to Europe and America.

Now, I have touched on this before, so there is no need for an in-depth response. But I have to say a few things in this connection.

Christianity comes from Christ, and means to be in Christ or to follow Him. The followers of Jesus were first called Christians in Antioch between the years 30-40 A.D. (see Acts 11:26). It began in the same part of the world that Judaism and Islam began—that is Asia or Asia Minor and Africa—all three of them trace their beginnings back to a man called Abraham. I have made the point that there is much evidence to support the claim that he was black.

In the first centuries the most influential theological schools were in North Africa. Christianity was not introduced into all of Africa by the white man. Some parts of Africa had already come under Christian influence long before the slave trade. The oldest church in Christendom isn't white, but black. It is the Coptic Church. (Copt is another word for Egypt.)

Now, just let me say a word about the so-called death or decay of Christianity. I thank God I have had occasion to travel. I have seen things with my own eyes and heard with my own ears. Therefore, what I say to you grows out of what I have seen and heard.

If I were able, I would put everybody on planes, boats, and buses and say, Go visit other countries, talk to people of other cultures, religions, and ideologies. For I think if people did travel, so much of the prejudice, hatred, and ignorance that exists among people would disappear. I have often thought that 95 percent of the untruths about other people—and people build their lives around these untruths—would be erased with travel.

In Africa, perhaps the most massive movement in the history of man is among what is called independent churches or indigenous churches. In South Africa, 14 percent is Pentecostal. It has been estimated that one-fifth of the population in Brazil is Pentecostal. There are revivals in Korea, Indonesia, and so on, and I will be quoting shortly from people of these and other countries. I have personally talked with Christian people from Burma, Vietnam, and Mozambique.

The proof is incontrovertible that Christianity has an African-Asian origin, and evidence grows in many parts of the world, especially in what have come to be called the Third World countries.

Now, if after studying the life and works of Jesus you want to reject Him, well, that's one thing. But to reject Jesus because of what someone with an axe to grind, or an organization to promote, says about Him, makes you immature and/or docile.

Now, there is no doubt that whites have used Christianity for their own purposes. In the name of Jesus they have done some abominable things. But then, so have blacks. In the name of Jesus, blacks sell numbers, dead prophets bones, blessed cabbages, and anything else poor gullible souls will buy.

If you want to be critical of how folks have used Jesus for their own personal ends, I can be as harsh and cutting as anybody. In fact, I can be sharper. I know first-hand more about the church and the followers of Jesus than most people. But we must always be careful that we don't repudiate the real in our rejection of the false. There is counterfeit money, but I don't see anybody rejecting the genuine. No one goes out and shoots the cow because somebody dilutes the milk for his own profit.

I have been privileged to converse with people from practically every religion and background, and I have come to the conclusion that few people reject Jesus because they have studied His life and works. Rather, I find that the rejections come from false information and impressions conveyed by the so-called followers of Jesus or His enemies, who feel they must tear Him down to build themselves up.

What we need to do is get to the source. If you sincerely want to learn about Jesus, go to the Bible yourself. Say in your heart, God, I want the truth about Jesus. Teach me. I urge this method upon you for that is the way that I became a Christian, and I have been a follower of Jesus for over twenty years.

I heard somebody say the other day, "Come on out of Christianity, it's the white man's religion." The truth is most of us have never been in Christianity in the first place. We have been the victims of the white man's use of Christianity. Few blacks, comparatively speaking, have been in Christianity, for to be in Christianity is, as I have pointed out, to be in Christ.

Now the next time you hear someone saying that Christianity is the white man's religion, he is either ignorant of the facts; or knows the facts, but is lying to you for his personal gain; or he means that white people have used Christianity for their own purposes. If that is what he is saying, then you have no argument with him. For to say that is to speak the truth, and it does not detract from the life and works of Jesus.

In any event you should always inquire from the man who says Christianity is the white man's religion, asking what does he mean?

Now, I want you to hear some of the most eloquent voices I have ever heard discuss the meaning of Jesus in their context.

India

Human suffering in all its forms is and has been for centuries, an overwhelming experience for India and has occupied a place at the center of its consciousness and its concerns. The nation's efforts are geared to mitigating and overcoming sorrow and pain with a view to securing an ever fuller life and greater dignity for the masses of India's men and women. Here comes alive, to Christians (and to others as well), with new relevance and significance, Jesus who healed the sick and fed the hungry, who came that we might have life in all its fullness. Jesus and His gospel are becoming a fresh incentive for us to work for human well being on earth. Meanwhile we are also struggling to understand suffering which is always with us in the shape of floods, droughts, cyclones, invasions, sickness, and death. For India's ancient insight that suffering has meaning in terms of refinement and deepening of the spirit has been infinitely enhanced by the mystery of Him who was exalted and made Christ Lord and Savior on account of his lowliness and obedience unto death on the cross. India has the cross, and we ask if it does not have also the Christ who makes all human suffering His own. We Christians are inclined to answer in the affirmative. When, in the post-war years, social problems and human suffering came, instead of the loves and wars of the rich, for serious treatment in Indian literature, it was discovered in some quarters, by leading non-Christian writers, that the only adequate symbol for dealing with the subject was the cross of Christ. And the person of Christ has been pointed to as the source and model of the selfless love and fearless action required to alleviate pain and change structures. Christ is coming more and more to be looked upon in India as a revolutionary figure who was ready to question and upset everything that stood in the way of the freedom and growth and well being of man, who God loves.

Cameroon

In experiencing the encounter with Jesus Christ, the African welcomes Christ as Son of God, in the mist of life and death, the one whom, by his life, teaching, miracles, suffering, death, and resurrection, is for man the supreme Master of Initiation, the one who knows the final truth about the meaning of life and the meaning of death, the one who brings the final victory of life over death. In the second place, the African also encounters Christ as Son of Man, making himself one of us. The mystery of the incarnation must be treated seriously. In time and space Christ takes our flesh, speaks our language, shares our lot in all its concrete everyday experiences. It is precisely here, in this concrete experience, that he demonstrates His victory over death, by healing the sick, by feeding the poor, by raising the dead, by pardoning sins, and finally conquering death by his own death and resurrection.

We respond to this Christ who became our brother as a family. We speak to Him in our own language and He answers us; we welcome Him with all that is best in our cultural heritage, our art, our music, our dances, our ornaments, our stored wisdom. We respond to Christ as a family; in other words, as a human community and as a cosmic community. In our confession of faith, in our worship, in the humble confession of our sins, and our joy in the salvation held out to us in Christ, we bring as it were an offering in praise of God, not only with the voice of the human community but also with the voice of the cosmos.

South Africa

Though, as an African, I can recognize myself in the preceding considerations, I cannot express my understanding of Jesus Christ in exactly these terms. I am living in another part of Africa and my cultural situation is more complex. For me, it is not just a matter of relating the gospel to a given traditional culture. I am confronted with social and political factors which have caused and are still causing tensions within that cultural milieu itself. Let me mention just a few of the elements which complicate my cultural situation:

1. The whites are playing a dominant role in the political and economic affairs of daily life. This has served to make white cultural values a more determining factor in the ordering of daily life than the traditional values.

2. The use of black workers through the system of migrant labor has broken up family life, which used to be one of the stabilizing factors in the traditional culture. This, coupled with the general exploitation of black labor has undermined the social and economic security of the black man and, as a result, has dehumanized him. Thus, the black man's culture cannot be looked upon in traditional terms. In order to understand the present cultural situation, the social, economic, and political factors must be taken into account. It is against the background of this complex network of factors that the vision of Christ as the fountain of hope in a hopeless situation has to emerge.

How do I see Jesus Christ?

1. I see him as the liberator of the black man from all that destroys and arrests the maturity of his "true humanity." To save in this context means to liberate. Thus salvation is liberation from inhumanity. This inhumanity encompasses more than just the broken personal relationship with God. It includes also a life of denial of the basic rights and facilities which account for the realization of the wholeness of life, e.g., economic, political rights, and other human rights.

2. Christ through forgiveness brings hope in a situation of despair. He reassures the nearness of God to the victims of oppression and social injustice. By taking their place in the sphere of humanity he gives them courage to be men and liberates them from fear, guilt and self-pity.

3. From this position of self-discovery in solidarity with Christ they gain courage to stand actively and creatively against the forces of oppression and exploitation, i.e., against the consequences of other people's sins."

Korea

There is need for a common strategy which transcends the limited interest of each part of the world. The situation of the world needs to be taken into account as we formulate the hope which has been revealed in Christ.

Though in Korea we are not lacking the values of the past providing the possibility of self-identification, our concern is more with our future. I am convinced that Christian identity must not be sought in the past, but in the future. I can try to define myself by my Confucian, Buddhist, or Shintoist past. But as a Christian I am striving for the future. We do not know yet what we shall turn out to be. We must not try to define ourselves by our "blackness" or by our "whiteness." But all of us must strive to become new men. In this sense, in my eyes, the present emphasis on the cultural values of the past means pushing people "back into the forest" instead of pulling them out of the forest in order to become new men.

I am making this plea for a common account of hope because I feel that the experience of my country and people point to the need of common expression of faith made by all Christians. I live in a place which, through the centuries, has been the victim of the international conflicts. We have suffered under brutal imperial invasion, we have suffered from the 19th-century colonialism, we have suffered from the totalitarianism of the early part of the 20th century, we have suffered from the ideological conflicts. We are the victims of international power politics. Being located in one of the hot spots of the international conflicts, we cannot help but look out for a common account of hope made by Christians. If the whole world has hope, then we can have hope. Any local expression of hope, any local victory of self-realization does not give us the hope we are waiting for. Only the hope of the whole world can give us hope.

I am only saying, comparing the world today with the world of the time of Jesus, there are reasons for hope. Real reasons, however, only if we accept our responsibility and as God's people work out the strategy which is required.

JESUS, THE SURPRISING CONTEMPORARY (C)

Last week I highlighted some contemporary thinking about Jesus. I mentioned that Christ, as seen through Indian eyes, was Christ the suffering servant finding profound relevance primarily because of India's suffering. I discussed a consideration of Jesus from the Cameroon, West Africa, where Jesus was seen as the fulfillment of culture. Then, from another part of Africa—namely, South Africa—Jesus was understood to be a liberator, the God who came to break down political and social structures that dehumanize; that God also came to liberate man to full humanity. And finally, I talked about a Korean approach which saw Jesus as a reconciler.

Jesus is contemporary because he meets us at our deepest needs. It is His ability not to be static or fixed in history and time, but to be dynamic and always relevant, always speaking to the present that, aside from His own followers, makes Him Lord of such a wide diversity of humanity.

But we must always give greater attention to the image or concept that the prevailing culture, leadership, or scholarship would make of Jesus. The selfishness and corruption of the human heart would have Jesus be that which promotes its own interest, to the neglect of others.

A few years ago, Cardinal Francis Joseph Spellman (Bishop of New York, 1939-67) wanted to make Jesus the blesser of bullets and bombs! Ideas about Jesus change from time to time and from culture to culture.

I believe that Jesus as liberator is far more appropriate to our times, than, shall we say, Jesus as shepherd, and that image would be in harmony with scripture. Or maybe another way of saying it is: Jesus as shepherd is appropriate for some people, but for others would be totally inadequate.

We should remember that the picture of God as a good shepherd, which we have loved so much, and which Psalm I recommend often, would be counterproductive in a culture where shepherds are seen as old men and women.

I believe today it is particularly the obligation of the Black minister to show Jesus as one who is black and angry, for Jesus has already been painted white. So, to say nothing is to leave things as they are. Falsehood is never rectified by the absence of action.

A sweet, gentle Jesus may be alright for some folks, but I think an angry Black Jesus with bushy hair, fire in his eyes, sword in his hand, and judgement in his voice would be a more appropriate image of Jesus. And yes, that Jesus would be a biblical Jesus also. For God has always shown Himself to be on the side of the outcasts, the dispossessed of the social order. Today, that would be blackness. Therefore, if God is consistent with Himself, He must be in blackness, and He must be angry.

I think any righteous man living today, seeing the poverty, the exploitation, the brutalization, is angry. If that be the case for man, think how much more it would be for God. The Bible says, "God is angry with the wicked everyday."

Now I know that what I have said bothers some people. But let us remember that Jesus Christ has left us a legacy of the incarnation, that is, God breaking into the history of humankind. Now, when God broke in, He did not come in a vacuum. He took upon Himself a form made in the likeness of man. And this Man had to express Himself in the thought patterns, the concepts, the ideas, imagination, and symbolisms of His time. Naturally, He could speak eternal truth, but He had to use the means of communication available to Him.

Now the world into which He came was a mixture of Roman law, Greek philosophy, and African-Asian mysticism and metaphysics. So we can expect that His ideas, which, though authoritative, were clothed in the aforementioned cultures.

Let us keep in mind that it was God who initiated the action. It was God who decided to express Himself in human form and in the language and culture of a particular point in time and history.

Now, I want us to see five concepts of Jesus that have been very dear to people through the years. Five ways in which Jesus was seen, understood, and appreciated. I don't want to convey the impression that these concepts of Jesus are contradictory, for they are not. They are, however, as we shall see, complimentary.

When all is said and done, the question that Jesus put to Peter will have to be answered by everyone of us individually. "What think ye of Christ?"

1. *Jesus as example.* One of the views about Jesus was that He was an example. "Christ also suffered for you," wrote Peter, "leaving you an example, that you should follow His steps" (I Peter 2:21).

   Jesus set an example we should reproduce. "Let this mind be in you which was also in Christ Jesus . . ." (Philippians 2:4). The best of humankind is not the example, for the best of men failed. But Jesus never fails.

2. *Jesus as illuminator.* Closely related to the view of Christ as an example is the idea of Jesus as the one who brings divine knowledge. He is a revealer of the mystery of God. "We have the light of the knowledge of the glory of God in the face of Jesus Christ" (II Corinthians 4:6).

   "He brings us the truth and the truth makes us free."

   "He brings life and immortality to light through the gospel" (II Timothy 1:10).

The early church loved to dwell on the knowledge, the illumination, the revelation that came through Jesus Christ.

Clement of Rome, one of the early church fathers, wrote,

We fix our gaze on the heights of heaven and through Him we see the reflection of His faultless and lofty countenance, through Him the eyes of our hearts were opened. Through Him our foolish and darkened understanding blossomed towards the light. Through Him the master willed that we should taste immortal knowledge. Through Him God called us from darkness to light, from ignorance to full knowledge of the glory of His name.

The wisdom of the ages is embodied in Jesus.

3. *Jesus as victor.* Another picture of the work of Jesus Christ in His life and death is that of a victor. This is the view that Jesus in His life and death and in His resurrection finally and utterly defeated the evil, demonic powers whose aim was to destroy mankind. This idea of Jesus as victor found ready listners in the world in which He came.

Jesus as victor found eager acceptance in a world thought to be infested with demons. He came to break the power of demons, to set men free from demonic powers. They did not confine the demonic activity to the spiritual, but demonic influence was at work through human beings.

4. *Jesus as the one who makes us one with God.* Another view of Jesus was that he opened the way that we might become one with God. Jesus became what we are that we might become what He is. Man through Jesus can be lifted out of his state into the very life of God. "As many as receive Him—to them God gave the right to be His sons" (John 1:12).

You will observe the influence of this view on my thinking. The coming of God into humanity, the incarnation, God breaking into history in the person of Jesus, to gather up history into Himself. He became like us that we might become like Him.

5. *Jesus as victim and sacrifice for the sins of mankind.* I will conclude by observing that a view of Jesus which probably has had the greatest number of adherents has been Jesus as propitiation or sacrificer for our sins.

Our next sermon will explore the various concepts which grew out of this view of Jesus.

JESUS, THE SURPRISING CONTEMPORARY (D)

We concluded the last sermon by looking at Jesus as the victim and the sacrificer for the sins of mankind. This concept of Jesus took five directions:

1. There is the idea that the death of Jesus is the ransom price paid for the liberation of men from the bondage in which he was held and from which he could never free himself.

> "The Son of Man," said Jesus, "came not to be served, but to serve, and to give His life a ransom for many" (Matthew 20:28).

> "There is one God, and one mediator between God and men, the man Christ Jesus; Who gave himself a ransom for all" (I Timothy 2:5-6).

> "You know you were ransomed from your futile ways, inherited from your fathers by tradition, not with perishable things like silver and gold but with the precious blood of Christ" (I Peter 1:18-19).

Again, the idea of ransom would be vivid to that society. David Smith points out in his book *The Atonement in the Light of History*:

> There could have been fewer more relevant pictures of the work of Christ, if that was to be stated in terms con-

> temporary with first century life . . . . This was the age of
> piracy; the traveler traveled in danger; at any time he
> might be captured and held for ransom, and a ransom had
> to be paid if his freedom was to be regained.
>
> There is no doubt, that in the early church the idea of
> divine ransom would speak to man's heart in terms which
> they knew and understood.

Jesus comes today to buy us back, to pay our debts. If we feel
imprisoned today, whatever the nature of the imprisonment, Jesus
comes to you as ransom. He is in this connection a redeemer.
One who buys back.

2. There is the idea that the death of Jesus is the sacrifice which
   atones for the sins of man.

   There is the general feeling that Jesus did something for me
   that I couldn't do for myself. This is not just one idea concerning
   the work of Jesus, but it lies at the core of all the concepts.
   Jesus was sent from heaven to do something for human beings,
   and while we may not be sure what it was exactly, still, He has
   done something with relationship to God which we could never
   have done on our own, and on this rests the whole message in
   the New Testament.

   This is the concept of the work of Jesus that shows the greatest Hebrew influence, while the deification of man, or the emphasis on the divinity of man, shows the greatest Greek influence.

   It would have been impossible for the Hebrew to express his
   idea of the work of Christ in any other way. The Israelites'
   religion was founded in the sacrificial system. It was founded on
   this system because it was founded on law. When God took it
   upon Himself to enter into a special relationship with the Hebrew people, that relationship was founded upon law.

   But it is the terrible predicament of man that he cannot keep
   the law. So, as often as he breaks it, he is guilty of transgres-
   sion. Now if the situation were left there, man would be irre-
   trievably lost. But it is the sacrificial system that came to the
   rescue. By the offering of animals, which God had ordained
   should be offered, the broken relationships could be restored.

This system said three things, I might add.

It said that man is a sinner, and his sinning is against God. It said also that to sin is a dreadful thing that costs the life of something—in this system, an animal. And finally it said that God is the only one who sets the condition for restoration. And it is here that the Grace of God comes in, as we shall see presently—the unmerited, undeserved favor of God to all humankind.

So man's relationship or covenant rests upon the sacrificial system. The Hebrews could readily see the connection between Jesus as the Lamb of God, and the Lamb offered in the sacrificial system to restore the covenant. When John looks up and sees Jesus coming, he says, "Behold the Lamb of God who taketh away the sins of the world" (John 1:29), and when Paul says, "God has made Him to be sin for us who knew no sin, that we might be the righteousness of God in Him" (II Corinthians 5:21), both of them would be clearly understood by their Hebrew contemporaries.

The word "lamb" also had the meaning of liberation. For the people were to slay a lamb and sprinkle the blood on the door, so that when the death angels went through the land of Egypt, they would past over them. They were covered by the blood. So when God led them out of bondage, they looked back and remembered that liberation came when the blood was applied.

Christ as lamb means liberation. He died that we might be liberated, made free. When we accept Him we are free!

3. In the third concept of the work of Jesus, we think of his work in terms of satisfaction. Bible students will see that there is no biblical basis for the terminology. The expression comes out of the medieval period of history. It is the time of chivalry and knighthood, and a scholar by the name of Anselm developed a concept of the work of Christ which bears the stamp of that age. Anselm, in a book written in 1098 called *Why God Became Man*, wrote:

> All creatures owe God perfect obedience. If that obedience were given there would be no sin. Sin is failure to give God what is owed Him; which is perfect submission to His will and law. Now to fail to give God what belongs

to Him is to take away from God what is His, therefore, insulting the honor of God.

And in an age of chivalry, it was the first principle that he, whose honor was belittled, or injured, sought satisfaction, "and so," said Anselm, "it was with God."

But why, even if God's honor is insulted, can not God just forgive the culprit? Why is satisfaction necessary? Because God is the moral governor of the universe, and if His honor can be insulted with impunity and without satisfaction, then the moral government of the universe is discredited. Hence, man must pay for violating the honor of God. But Jesus comes and voluntarily takes upon Himself the punishment that is due man, and since Jesus' life is perfect, He can do this. So, the honor of God is satisfied.

4. The fourth interpretation of the work of Jesus is seen as substitution. This is the concept upon which the Reformation laid great stress. It is very similar to the satisfaction concept. God is king of the universe who rightfully requires man's loyalty. But man is a sinner and rebels against God, hence, he stands condemned. There is nothing that man can do for himself. His soul is comparable to that of a convicted murderer in prison. The offender can sweep the floors and wash the walls, but he is still in prison with the death penalty hanging over his head.

Now into this situation comes Jesus. He takes the murderer's place in prison, then goes to the death house. Man is free to leave on one condition, that he gives his life to the one who died for him. The penalty of his sins has been borne by another. This is Paul's statement, "God has made Him to bear sin for us." This view says that on the cross Jesus Christ bore the penalty and punishment for sin and that He did so as an act of voluntary, spontaneous, and sacrificial love.

5. This final concept about Jesus is called the moral influence. It says simply that Jesus Christ came to proclaim, to demonstrate, and to exhibit the love of God; to say in His life and death for men, God loves you like that. He came to tell people that they are sinners but already forgiven sinners, if they will accept the love of God.

Now let me talk about a covenant. Paul quotes Jesus as saying, "This cup is the new covenant in my blood" (I Corinthians 11:25).

A covenant is a relationship entered into by two people. The difference between the covenant entered into by human beings and the covenant entered into by God is that in the case of human beings, it is a covenant of equals. But with God, it is an agreement between unequals. Therefore, the whole initiative rests with God. Now we have seen that in the Old Testament, this covenant was founded upon the sacrificial system. The agreement remained intact as long as man was obedient, which he never was. Then, to restore the relationship, animals were offered. But now, there is mention made of a new covenant. Jeremiah had hinted as much over 600 years before Christ. He said there would be a covenant made not of the keeping of external laws, but it would be written on the heart and inward parts. The new covenant would be built upon love and devotion of the heart and there is no mention of sacrifice at all.

Notice that both Jeremiah and Paul talked about a new covenant, and both use the same Greek words for the new. Now there are two Greek words for new. One is *neos*, which is "newness" in a point of time. A thing is *neos* when it is the latest of its kind. But then there is *kanios*, which means "newness" altogether. It means that a new quality has entered into life.

Now the word that both Jeremiah and Paul used with reference to covenant is *kanios*. It is a new covenant, introducing an altogether new idea into the world. This newness is not a revision or renewing of the old, for that would be *neos*, but this is a newness, *kanios*; God is going to do a totally new thing— and what is it? It is that the relationship between God and man will no longer rest upon the sacrificial system, no longer rest upon externally imposed laws, but will rest upon love and the heart. People will be accounted righteous by their love of God, drawn from them voluntarily.

And how is this to be done? That brings us to this. Remember that Jesus said, "This new covenant came at the price of My blood." What Jesus was saying is that this new kind of covenant is made possible only at the cost and at the price of His life. When we put it all together we see that Jesus is saying that the new relationships between man and God is made possible through His blood; that is, through His life and death.

To conclude then, we are driven back to answer the question that Jesus put to His disciples: "What think ye of Christ?"

JESUS, THE SURPRISING CONTEMPORARY (E)

The Question that I am asking today is, Where shall we find Jesus today?

Let me try to state what I have said thus far. I have said that Jesus is always a contemporary because He meets us where we are—in the boundless nature of His work, His message, and the relevance in which He disposes Himself in our culture and in our age.

I touched upon some contemporary thinking about Jesus from different countries. From India, Jesus, the high point of God's self-manifestation is contemporary because He has known suffering. In the Cameroon, West Africa, Jesus is contemporary as He fulfills the highest cultural aspirations that were hinted at during the old rituals. In South Africa, Jesus is contemporary because He comes as liberator, as one who shatters the political and economical social structures that dehumanize, and provides a full humanity. In Korea, Jesus is reconciler. He heals the brokenness of the human family as well as the brokenness between man and God.

Then I sought to show that, through history, different aspects of the work and life of Jesus were emphasized according to the need, the cultural understanding and so on. Jesus has been seen as example, as illuminator, as victor over all evils, as deifier of man, as victim and sacrifice (offering Himself as ransom, sacrifice, satisfaction, substitution), and He has been seen as the one who came to manifest the love of God.

I pointed out that Jesus came to introduce a new covenant. I said that newness here is from a Greek work "*kanios,*" which means "newness" in terms of a new concept, a new process. It is not a newness in point of time, the latest thing to happen; not a rehashing of the old, but newness in terms of quality and kind. This new covenant then had to do with man's relationship to God.

Jesus came to show that the covenant now would rest upon the devotion of the heart and not upon sacrificial systems, and that this covenant came at the price of His blood. Because of His death, people could say God loves like that, and they would love God in return. Love would be the fulfillment of all law; love of God and love of neighbor. In this new covenant one served and obeyed not through any rigid adherence to laws and codes, but through love.

I said that this was what put Jesus on collision course with the power that was. Rituals, ceremonies, and laws were meaningful to Jesus to the extent that they enlarged the life of humankind; but to the extent that they stifled and stunted growth and fulfillment, they were to be discarded. And since the then-existing society rested upon adherence to animal sacrifices, codes, do's and don'ts, self-identity and prestige and respectability were wrapped in these things. Jesus would have the choice of conforming or the cross. He chose the cross.

I have said that I thought that the Jesus we need is one who comes in blackness, and blackness here symbolizes what white society has come to call "nothingness." Blackness covers all who are despised—the dehumanized, the exploited; and in that sense, it also covers the Hispanics, Indians, Asians, and Africans. Yes, even the "poor whites" who have committed themselves to the cause of blackness.

I have said that the God of our faith has always shown Himself to be for the down-and-outers, the misfits, and ne'er-do-wells. Therefore, if He is to be consistent with Himself, He must come to us as He came in the person of Jesus, over 1900 years ago—despised, deprived, and persecuted. He must come to us as He identified Himself with the nation of Israel, a people enslaved, with the oppressor's boot on their necks. God was not ashamed to say to this nation of slaves, You are my people, I will bring you out of bondage; I will come in the person of Moses; I will liberate you and you shall worship me on this mountain; you shall celebrate my liberation. So, we look for Jesus again, but where shall we locate Him.

If you look to whiteness you will not find Him there. Now, I mean whiteness as a symbol; just as blackness has always meant nothingness in this society, whiteness has always meant everythingness. Whiteness is more than a color, it is a value system; it is a certain mentality; it's a lifestyle; it's a frame of reference; it's an attitude; it's availability of advantages; it's membership in the clubs; it's automatic inclusion in the American systems, it's a way of life; it is Nixon in the White House, Governor Nelson Rockefeller (state of New York) in Albany, and John Lindsay (mayor of New York) downtown at City Hall; it is the control of the educational system; it is control of the medical institutions, the banking system; it is the creator and sustainer of the ghettoes in America and in other parts of the world; it is arrogance; it is Jesus, God, the Saints and anybody else of any worth. For if a person isn't white in color, and he achieves anything—he is made white in his values, his lifestyles, his frame of reference—the chances are very slim that he can be an achiever in this society without becoming white.

And there was a time when it was acceptable to try to be white. Negroes did everything they could to be white. They straightened their hair or wore wigs; bought skin-whiteners; boasted about their white friends and white wives and husbands. Look at poor Sammy Davis: a man of tremendous ability, he allowed himself to be reduced to being Sinatra's little sambo and Nixon's little nigger.

Nowadays, one tries to be white on the sneak. He is black by day when he is with black people, then gets into whiteness later on. For he knows that if he is going to get the material prosperity he desires, he has to do some imitations. But that's not so bad as long as he knows where his real identity is.

Moses is an example here. He was raised in the pharaoh's house, he went to pharaoh's school, he learned all of pharaoh's tricks; but he always remembered who he was. He didn't lose his identity in the Pharaoh's house. For the day came when he was chosen by God to lead the people to freedom.

Let us remember that you are not what you are until you say that's what you are, and world conditions are meaningless until you internalize them. You can live anywhere, work anywhere, and so long as your mind is positive and right, you will be the one influencing and not being influenced.

So now, if you're looking for Jesus, it isn't likely you're going to find him in the White House, no matter how many times the president says, God bless you. It isn't likely you're going to find him amongst the bankers and insurance companies. You're not going to find Him in the offices of huge corporations. You're not going to find Him in Congress, no matter how many congressional prayer meetings are held. For the existing mind set in those places is anti-God, antirighteous, and antijustice. The God of our faith is on record as opposing those who practice injustice.

It's very interesting that white theologians a few years ago began to inform the world that God was dead. Paul Van Buren, a professor of theology at the Episcopal Theological Seminary wrote, "God has died of neglect, a quiet displacement has taken place." William Hamilton, another theologian at Colgate Rochester Divinity School wrote, "I am here referring to a belief in the non-existence of God. When we speak of the 'death of God," we speak not only of the death of idols, we speak as well of the death in us of any power to affirm any of the traditional images of God. I mean that the world is not God and that it does not point to God." In another place he said, "We are not talking about the absence of the experience of God but about the experience of the absence of God."

Now, what is the meaning there? To me the death of God is a contradiction—for if He is God, He cannot die. If he died, He could not have been God. He was an impostor. It seems to me that the problem with these theologians is that they had located God in the wrong places. They had thought that God was synonymous with the white culture; that God and the flag were one; that white politics, white economics, white values were one with God. In a word, they thought, as many others thought and still think, that God and whiteness are one and the same thing.

But then they discovered that the name of God was being harnessed to every conceivable kind of oppression, dehumanization, and those who talked about God didn't really believe in Him, at least not the God of justice and truth. And so, it became obvious that God had become a game. And then with technological development, whites didn't need to invoke the name of God anymore. Why, they were God themselves.

So, it became obvious to them that God must have died. But the truth of the matter is, He never lived in their style, political system, churches, or cathedrals. God was never there. At least, not the God of our faith.

Now, it is significant that even our black forefathers, during slavery, without any formal education, knew that the God of the Bible and the God of the slavemaster weren't the same one. So what uninformed blacks in the most deplorable condition knew, and scholars and theologians and preachers were ignorant of, is that God was not in the big house on the hill; that God was not in the slave traffic; but God was in the slave hut, there amongst the bleeding black bodies of the slaves.

And when they talked about God, they weren't playing games with words. Talking about God, or God talk, as the white theologians called it, and they say that's useless too, wasn't an exercise in proper grammar or exquisite English, but talking about God was a matter of life and death.

Jesus as the surprising contemporary is found amongst the outcasts of the earth. And also among the rich and powerful who have seen the illusion of these things, or who are using their resources in the furtherance of God's kingdom.

The End of Compartmentalization

There is another dimension that we need to add to make the picture complete. Evangelical Christians and others have sought to divide social action and spiritual action. However, in the scripture that depicts Jesus in the temple (Matthew 21:12-14) we discover the beginning of the solution to the compartmentalization problem.

There, in these verses, we see Jesus move from a furious assault upon the money changers to healing the sick and lame. There is no dichotomy in Jesus' behavior. He confronts exploitation and at the same time, in the same place, comforts the victims. He is a condemner and a consoler. Thus, in spite of what religionists say, even the most well-intentioned, regarding the need to separate the social from the spiritual, radical social action and personal religion, Jesus gave us the example.

Christians must be prophetic as well as pastoral. There is an Old Testament example in the Book of Isaiah. The prophet is seen going to advise King Hezekiah regarding the threats of Assyria (Isaiah 37:21-38). Then we see the prophet again in the sick room of King Hezekiah assuring him that God had heard his prayers (Isaiah 38). In the next chapter Isaiah is back in the royal court again, this time warning the King about the Babylonians (Isaiah

39). Isaiah, like Jesus, moves from one kind of action—political involvement at the highest level—to minister to the sick; from the royal court to the room of the ill.

Yet, why it should have been thought otherwise must be attributed to European worldview or stratagem. Compartmentalization of the social and the spiritual is absent in African worldview, and it is unsound biblically. The God of our faith is presented as the Creator who is intensely concerned about the total person. Even the strands of our hair are numbered (Luke 12:7).

The sparrow cannot fall to the ground without His notice (Matthew 10:29-31).

JESUS, THE SURPRISING CONTEMPORARY CONCLUSION

In the presence of this Jesus, who can turn away? The only ones who should have problems with this Jesus are the exploiters and oppressors. They will always try to co-opt Him, or crucify Him. And those who truly follow Him can expect the same treatment. But for the common people in every age, Jesus Christ, stripped of the cultural distortion, has always had an irresistible appeal. It was this Jesus, lost amid the wrappings of European imagery and passivity, from whom innumerable Black people turned away.

The mission that many Black theologians and churchmen saw for themselves was to divest Jesus of Europeanization and thus allow Him to stand forth in all His biblical truth. For those who understood this mission, who braved the loneliness and criticism, they can rightfully receive their accolades.

They have said to their Black brothers and sisters, particularly their youth, Here is Jesus. He is not a namby-pamby, wishy-washy European. He does not take sides with the oppressor. But He is strong, courageous, African in origin, against exploitation and oppression, and for the poor and wretched. His Spirit lives today, seeking to inhabit human bodies to empower them to live victoriously.

If there be those who would argue that there should be no color with Jesus, our answer is, We agree. There should be none. But, unfortunately, there is. This is a racist society, and we did not make it that way. Given that fact, then, we cannot leave the color question alone; for to do so is to perpetuate the existing order. A deliberate effort was made by whites to make whiteness superior. Blacks must make a deliberate effort to at least tell the truth regarding color, especially as it relates to religion.

Moreover, it is a biblical principle that one always begins with one's own people. Jesus said at one point. "I am not sent but to the lost sheep of the House of Israel (Matthew 10:5, 6; 15:22-24)." Paul also praised his cultural credentials (Philippians 3:4-11). But in each case both moved from particularity to universality. Jesus later said, "Go you therefore and teach all nations ...." (Matthew 28:18-20). Paul said, "What things were gain to me, I count loss for the excellency of the knowledge of Jesus Christ." The first-century Jewish spiritual leader Rabbi Hillel said, "If I am not for myself, who will be for me? If I am only for myself, what am I? If not now, when?"

To say to an oppressed people, whose color had been used against them, Your God is not the color of those who have oppressed you but He is your color. Nor does He side with their actions. He is against their actions and He is on your side and has already made you conqueror— to say that is not racist, nor is it to speak against any people. It is, first of all, to tell the truth. Second, it is, to tell the truth to a people who have been robbed of their history, made to hate themselves and become slaves and pawns, and to serve everybody's interest but their own. Nor should anyone be threatened by the truth. To be threatened is to make suspect the sincerity of whites, rather than Blacks.

If whites were truly saved or committed to Jesus, they would rejoice in Black discovery of the truth and even more with Blacks' internalization of the truth. But it should be emphasized that white attitudes ought not to influence anything one way or the other. Perhaps too much time has been spent on the subject already.

If Blacks become too preoccupied with white people's thinking, they have still not liberated themselves. They are like the people in a testimony meeting who arise to give a testimony praising God and end up spending 90 percent of the time talking about the devil.

Blacks should say to whites, We have found the real Jesus, and He has set us free. We do not hate you, but we do love ourselves, and because we love ourselves, we are more inclined to love you, for we understand that he who truly loves himself cannot hate another. We are not against you, but we are against exploitation and oppression and we are determined to struggle against these conditions. Now what you do with our self-love is your responsibility, and we will not spend valuable time worrying about what your attitudes and/or actions are going to be.

Again, we say to people of African descent, and indeed to all people, *Here is Jesus the Christ, African in origin— revolutionary and redeeming in action—Hear and follow Him!*

Index